"Finally, family devotions for teens that are extremely creative, absolutely practical, biblically sound and yet unusually amusing. *Bashed Burritos, Green Eggs* . . . hits the bull's eye, and with it, parents can't miss."

—**Pastor Bill Reed**, regional minister,
Great Lakes District, Evangelical Free Church of America

"This book is excellent and will be an asset to all who read it. As a grandpa, I am personally excited about *Bashed Burritos, Green Eggs.* . . . I think it should be in every grandparent's library as a tool to share stories from God's Word."

—**Brian Ogne**, president,
Timber-lee Ministries, WI

"What this book contains is the 'how-to' that many parents need for 'training their children in the way they should go. . . .' *Bashed Burritos, Green Eggs* . . . is not just fluff; it's easy to follow and fun. In addition to parents, any children's ministry leader could successfully use this book for their classes."

—**Mary Kay Meeker**, adult/family ministries director
(former youth camp director), Timber-lee Christian Center, WI

"In this book, Tim and Cheryl present creative, hands-on activities and illustrations that teach biblical principles for practical application in daily Christian living."

—**Richard E. Carlson**, director,
Camp Awana, Chicago, IL

"Tim and Cheryl Shoemaker write as people who have been in the trenches with kids for some time. They understand how to grab the attention of those very special persons we call adolescents and make Scripture real in their lives. . . . I highly recommend his latest book, *Bashed Burritos, Green Eggs.* . . . It will be a blessing not only for your youth group at church but for those of us who grapple with how we can impart eternal truth to our young people at home as well."

—**Dwight A. Perry, Ph.D.**, professor of pastoral studies,
Moody Bible Institute, IL

"I love this book! Spiritual leadership starts at home, and this book gets you started in a fun, fresh way. Jump in and immerse yourself with new and refreshing ideas for family ministry. Mom, Dad, Grandma—this book is for you! Godly principles presented in dynamic, creative ways. Your kids will love them!"

—**Pastor Jim Condap**, pastor to students,
Evangelical Covenant Church, Easton, CT

Bashed Burritos, Green Eggs
. . . and Other Indoor/Outdoor Devotionals
You Can Do With Your Kids

Tim and Cheryl Shoemaker

CHRISTIAN PUBLICATIONS, INC.
CAMP HILL, PENNSYLVANIA

✠ CHRISTIAN PUBLICATIONS, INC.

3825 Hartzdale Drive, Camp Hill, PA 17011
www.christianpublications.com

Faithful, biblical publishing since 1883

Bashed Burritos, Green Eggs . . . and Other Indoor/Outdoor
Devotionals You Can Do With Your Kids
ISBN: 0-87509-990-4
© 2004 by Tim and Cheryl Shoemaker
All rights reserved
Printed in the United States of America

04 05 06 07 08   5 4 3 2 1

Dedication

To our parents, Fred and Alice Beck
and Dick and Sylvia Shoemaker;
thank you for demonstrating a
Christlike love to us while we were growing up,
and for encouraging us to love God and serve Him.

Contents

Love is patient, love is kind. It does not envy, it does not boast, it is not proud. It is not rude, it is not self-seeking, it is not easily angered, it keeps no record of wrongs. Love does not delight in evil but rejoices with the truth. It always protects, always trusts, always hopes, always perseveres. Love never fails. (1 Corinthians 13:4-8)

OUTDOOR DEVOTIONALS

"You Expect <u>Me</u> to Lead Family Devotions?"

You're too busy. You're too tired. You're not qualified. You really don't enjoy doing this kind of stuff. You don't know if the kids will really like it . . . what if they get bored? You can think of plenty of reasons not to lead family devotions, can't you?

Let us give you one reason why you *should* lead family devotions: the kids. Our kids need every bit of help they can get to make it safely through the teenage years in today's corrupt culture.

It makes no difference if you're a dad or a mom, if you're a single parent or a grandparent. You need to do this for the kids.

In *Bashed Burritos, Green Eggs . . .* we tackle some tough topics in a fun way. We take the elements of love as described in First Corinthians 13 and help the kids understand how to really love others in practical ways. There are things in this book that the kids need to hear from you—just take a look at the table of contents. We even tackle some critical issues like premarital sex and pornography in a couple of the devotionals.

You *can* do this. Flip through a few pages and take a look at the format of one of the devotionals. This book is different from other devotional books you may have tried before. It is written in a "coaching" format that's almost like having us there helping and encouraging you along as you lead the kids. You don't have to memorize any part of the devotional. The book is designed to be your guide as you do the weekly devotions. Still unsure? Take a look at the How to Use This Book section for some practical help and you'll see that you really can do this.

If you use this book to help you lead your family devotions, the kids will actually enjoy them. Sounds impossible, right? Trust us. We tested our devotionals on our own three teenage boys (I wish you could have seen our sons' faces when we did Micro-Mess), and we can guarantee that kids won't dread these.

Ever since the day your child was born you've been making sacrifices for him or her, haven't you? Well, don't stop. You may have tried family devotions before and you aren't anxious to go there again. Do it anyway. You won't regret it.

—Tim and Cheryl Shoemaker

How to Use This Book

1. *Plan ahead.* These family devoes are designed to be done once a week. The key is to do them well, and that takes a little bit of preparation. Read the devoes for the upcoming week well ahead of time. Sometimes you'll have to pick up some supplies or make some arrangements in advance.

2. *Let the book be your guide.* The parts written in the skinny font (this one) are just for you. That's where we play "coach" to help you through the devotional. And don't think you need to memorize the lesson either. When we're leading family devoes, we always have our notes in front of us, just like they're written in this book.

3. *Keep your family devotional time short.* Most of the time there will be some kind of object lesson or activity to do before you actually tie the devotional together with some real teaching. It's OK to extend the activity time if the kids are really enjoying it, but you want to hold your teaching time to about ten minutes. Less is more. You need to resist the tendency to "preach." This is extremely important. If you start going longer, you'll bore the kids. Once they're bored, your job gets a lot tougher. If you keep it short, the kids are less likely to tune you out.

4. *Personalize the devoes.* Gear them to the age of your kids. The devotions in this book work well for kids from ages twelve to seventeen. If you need to customize things a bit, go ahead and do it. As you read the devotional in advance, you may see some areas where you'd like to slip in a personal example that will help illustrate the point of the lesson. That's great. That will make your devoes that much better.

5. *Don't let the little problems discourage you.* OK, you will get discouraged from time to time, but keep going. It will get better. If you miss a week, don't beat yourself up over it. Just get back on track as soon as you can. If the kids don't seem to be paying attention, don't be fooled; they hear everything you say. Are they fooling around too much? Don't get upset. Roll with it; join in the fun. It's a sign that they're enjoying devotions—and that's good news!

6. *Hang in there!* Sometimes leading family devotions can be tough. But remember, sometimes you have to do something you don't like to protect something you love. You love your kids, and you need to protect them by helping them prepare for the battles of life. One way you do this is by teaching them important biblical truths in family devotional time.

As you get a few of these devotionals under your belt, you'll find that leading family devoes isn't so bad after all. The kids will enjoy them, even look forward to them. The best thing is that you're helping them prepare for life in some awfully important areas. You'll never regret the effort you made to have family devotions.

C'mon. Give this book a try. You can do it!

INDOOR DEVOTIONALS

Micro-Mess

What's the Point?

Allowing sin and evil in our lives affects us from the inside out. We may not look like it from the outside, but we're definitely "cooking" ourselves inside. An egg in the microwave will help the kids see just how messy that can get.

Things You'll Need

- An uncooked egg in the shell (with some extras on hand, just in case)

- A heavy-duty, clear glass bowl (Pyrex would be a good choice for this)

- Several heavy plates or something of similar weight that will sit on top of the bowl

- A piece of paper and a pen for each kid

- A microwave (borrow one from a friend or neighbor if you don't have one)

Don't let the word mess *in the title keep you from doing this one. If you have boys, they'll love it. If you have girls, consider this a great opportunity to demonstrate why we don't microwave eggs in their shells. If you have both boys and girls, you can't miss.*

You'll need at least one egg for this one. The kids may want to do the activity more than once, so have some extra eggs on hand. You'll want a piece of paper and a pen for each of the kids so they can make "observations" as you go along.

Here We Go

You need to try this activity first. Yep, before you get the kids together, and preferably when they aren't home, try "nuking" an egg on your own. I imagine every microwave is different, so you'll want to know how yours reacts.

I took an egg right out of the fridge and put it in a thick glass bowl. I covered it with a heavy stoneware plate and set the timer for five minutes. I had just stepped out of the room for something when I heard a loud "woomphh." It had taken about two minutes for the egg to explode. The stoneware plate even lifted off the top, leaving scrambled-egg shrapnel all over the inside of the microwave. I learned two things: First, this was really fun, and second, next time I'll stack a couple more plates on top.

Once you've tested things out and cleaned any stray egg bits out of your microwave, you're ready to call in the troops. You might start out by saying something like this:

All right, kids, you're going to help me do a little experiment here. I'd like one of you to get an egg out of the fridge and put it in this glass bowl. We're going to cover it and put it in the microwave for five minutes. Are we clear so far?

If your kids are anything like ours, their pulses just increased a bit. They're probably pretty sure you aren't supposed to microwave eggs, so the fact that you're telling them to do it probably has them intrigued. One of the kids may even try to warn you that something bad might happen to the egg. Thank him, but explain that you're going to find out what happens firsthand. My guess is your kids won't warn you; they'll want to see the show.

Now, each of you will have a pen and paper. You'll be observing what happens in the microwave and recording it. Every fifteen seconds I'll say "time" and you guys will write down your observations. If you see no significant change, simply jot the letters NC on your paper to signify "no change." Any questions?

They'll be eager to get going, so you'll have to keep moving so you don't frustrate them. Hand out the paper and pens. Get the egg in the bowl, place it in the microwave and close the door.

Take just a second to check where the kids are. Don't let them get too close. You don't want anybody pressing his or her nose up against the window on this one. We set up chairs for the kids about five feet away from the microwave. You might ask one of the kids to set the timer to five minutes and press the start button.

Now, glance at your watch and call out "time" every fifteen seconds. The kids should scribble down a "NC" for no change at each fifteen-second interval. If they have any idea that the egg might explode, the tension will definitely be mounting. When the two-minute mark approaches, try not to give anything away. Keep a straight face so that the kids can't be quite sure if what they're expecting will happen. Even if they are expecting it, the egg suddenly bursting will catch them by surprise. They'll love it!

Once the egg has exploded, open the microwave. Be careful—the egg crumbs will be hot. Give everything about thirty seconds or so to cool down and then let the kids examine the scraps of egg plastered inside the bowl. There's a good chance that they'll want to do it again. That's fine, but I'd finish the devoes first. Then, after you've made the application, go ahead and blow up some more eggs. It will be a great way to reinforce the truth of what you'll be telling them.

After they've examined the mess, you might have them sit back down at the table and start off with something like this:

Now, that's why we don't microwave eggs. There was, however, a good reason we did it this time. I'll explain in a minute, but first tell

Avoiding a Meltdown

I don't need to tell you that none of these items should be made of metal, do I? Well, don't do it. The ensuing sparks are admittedly cool-looking and the kids would probably think it was great, but it isn't very good for the microwave.

me about your observations. Tell me what you noticed the first fifteen seconds, and the second and the third.

Get their input. You should get a bunch of "no change" responses. Perfect.

OK, so we see the egg had no visible change at first, and then suddenly "boom!" it wallpapered the bowl, right? So, if nothing was happening, why did it just blow up like that?

We're leading them to the answer we're looking for. If they give it to you, great. If not, no big deal. Just move on.

Just because the egg didn't appear to be affected by the microwave, it didn't mean it wasn't being cooked. To a casual observer, it almost seemed like the egg could stand the heat. The problem was, the microwave was cooking it from the inside out. The egg looked fine, but inside there were some definite changes going on.

In real life, sin has the same kind of result. We can allow some sin in without looking any different in the mirror. Like an egg in the microwave, sin cooks us from the inside out.

Let's listen to a few verses from the Bible:

> My son, pay attention to what I say;
>   listen closely to my words.
> Do not let them out of your sight,
>   keep them within your heart;
> for they are life to those who find them
>   and health to a man's whole body.
> Above all else, guard your heart,
>   for it is the wellspring of life.
>   (Proverbs 4:20-23)

> Therefore, get rid of all moral filth and the
> evil that is so prevalent and humbly accept

the word planted in you, which can save you. (James 1:21)

Dear friend, do not imitate what is evil but what is good. (3 John 11)

Tie It Together

Name some ways that other kids, maybe even Christian kids you know, allow sin to creep into their lives.

You've been doing all the talking for the last couple of minutes, so you need to get them engaged again. You're asking how "other" kids let sin into their lives. That's a lot less threatening than asking your kids how they let sin into their own lives. You may still get a glimpse at what your kids are allowing. Be quick to listen and slow to speak here.

Sometimes we flirt with sin just by what we choose to see on TV or at the movies. There can be a subtle corruption that takes place in our lives. Sometimes we're acting one way at church or home and another at school.

Sometimes we act like we're real angels, but it's a cover for some not-so-angelic things going on inside us. That's what the Pharisees did in their day. Jesus called them hypocrites, snakes and whitewashed tombs. That "whitewashed tombs" comment meant that they looked good on the outside, but inside the corruption was growing until it burst into open lies, deception and murder.

You can allow things in your life that shouldn't be there, things like pride, greed, rebellion, dishonesty, hypocrisy and others. You can be involved in sin that you think you can handle or cover up. You can look in the mirror and appear just the same as you always were. You must remember, though, that sin affects the heart, and if you let it stay in your life, it will cook you from the inside out.

That's why God warns us to guard our hearts. The sin we let in often enslaves us long before we even realize it. That's a scary thought, but it's right there in Proverbs 5:21-23.

It's probably a good idea to read those verses out loud, or you could give the kids an "assignment" to look them up later.

Once in a while you'll hear of a great man, a Christian or maybe a high-profile person, who suddenly is caught in some big sin. People are shocked because the person always seemed to possess real integrity. The fact is, that person is just another egg that blew up. That person allowed sin inside, and it was cooking him until, to everyone's surprise, it finally burst out.

Solomon was the wisest man who ever lived, and somehow he thought he could compromise with evil. He had a lot of wives, and they turned his heart from God. If the wisest man who ever lived couldn't escape the effects of sin, then it's a pretty good bet that we can't either.

People know that an egg in its shell can't be cooked in a microwave without blowing up. That's why nobody cooks eggs that way. It's dangerous. When it comes to sin, people know that allowing it in their lives is dangerous too, yet they do it anyway. Since we know that sin cooks us from the inside, we should try to see how far we can stay away from sin.

Somebody once said, "The only thing harder than living in this world is living in two worlds." I think what he meant was that living as a Christian in this world can be hard, but not as hard as trying to live like a Christian sometimes, and like a sinner other times. A double life like that is definitely living in the microwave.

My desire for you is that you protect your heart(s). Avoid evil. You can't escape its long-term effects. You need to follow God with a whole heart. Sometimes you're going to want my help with that. I'm not perfect, but I can help you if you find yourself struggling at some point. Talk to me, talk to the Lord, but don't let sin just sit there cooking you, OK?

Fight the urge to talk too much here. Try to notice if any of the kids seems to be struggling. Maybe they'll want to talk to you privately. Be sure to allow an opportunity for that.

You may want to microwave another egg or two now. The kids will enjoy it, and it will help etch the truth of the lesson on their hearts and minds.

Working It into the Week

Here are some passages that may be helpful for the kids to read during the week.

Day 1: Mark 7:6-8

Day 2: Proverbs 1:8-10; 3 John 11

Day 3: Proverbs 4:18-27

Day 4: Colossians 3:5-17; 1 Thessalonians 5:21-22

Day 5: Proverbs 5:21-23, 2 Timothy 2:22

Day 6: 1 Corinthians 13:4-7, 1 John 1:9

Green Eggs and Ham Scam

What's the Point?

A green meal isn't very appetizing, but it's basically harmless to eat. There is something else we refer to as "green" that we ingest all the time, but it truly is deadly: envy.

Things You'll Need

- Green liquid food coloring

- A meal comprised of foods that will absorb the food coloring well

Remember, a little food coloring goes a long way. The idea is to make an unnaturally green meal for the family. Sure, you could use vegetables that are already green, but that won't bring out the point as well.

We chose scrambled eggs and french toast because green food coloring mixes in well with both of them. You could put green food coloring in the milk you serve. You could even mix it into the butter for their toast. Green corn meal muffins would be a nice touch too. Instead of french toast, you may want to put a slab of ham with the eggs to tie into the classic children's book by Dr. Seuss, Green Eggs and Ham.

Or, you may want to come up with a completely different meal, depending on when devotions will work best into your family's schedule. Rice, mashed potatoes and cream-based sauces all absorb food coloring well. Go ahead and get creative on this—the more memorable the meal, the better the lesson will stick in the kids' minds.

Here We Go

Serve the family your green meal. How you explain the strange color of the food to the curious kids is up to you. With teenagers, there's no telling what to expect. Some may say they like it like that. Others may sullenly refuse to eat. Roll with it. You can tell them that it will all make sense after devoes tonight.

When you're ready to start devoes, you might start out by saying something like this:

OK, so you're probably wondering why I made the green meal today. I wanted to make a little point. The green food may not have looked very appetizing, but it was harmless to eat it. However, there's something else we often refer to as green, but if it gets inside us, it's very dangerous. Anybody have an idea of what I'm talking about?

Give them just a moment to think, then give them the answer.

I'm referring to envy or jealousy. Give me some examples of jealousy or envy you've seen in other kids you know.

They may be reluctant to give examples here, or they may not be able to come up with examples off the top of their heads like this. Be ready with a few examples of your own. Your examples could be something from when you were their age, something you observed in someone more recently or maybe something you read in the newspaper. After a few examples have been brought up, go ahead and move on.

Allowing envy or jealousy into our lives is very easy. Jealousy is very subtle. It creeps in quietly, almost unnoticed. We don't pay any attention to it, but that doesn't mean it's harmless. No, it's like a cancer that will consume us if we don't do a little surgery and get rid of it.

Can you think of any Bible characters that had a problem with envy or jealousy?

Let them think here. Hopefully they'll come up with something. If not, be ready to offer some examples like:

- Cain: envious of Abel's offering being accepted by God (see Genesis 4)

- Saul: jealous of David's popularity with the people (see 1 Samuel 18)

- Sarai: jealous of her servant's ability to have a child (see Genesis 16)

- Martha: jealous of her sister's time with Jesus (see Luke 10: 38-42)

- Pharisees: jealous of Jesus' power and popularity with the people (see Matthew 27:18)

As a result of the jealousy on the part of the people we just talked about, what kinds of things happened?

We want them to think about the effects jealousy has on a person and those around him. Add to their list if needed. Here's the list we looked at a minute ago.

- Cain: killed his brother

- Saul: tried to kill his loyal servant, David; alienated his own son; weakened his kingdom and authority

- Sarai: had her husband kick the servant and her child out; caused a conflict that still rages between nations

- Martha: she complained to Jesus; He put her in her place

You may want to consider a dessert to have after devotions. Maybe cupcakes with green frosting or lime sherbet. You could make sugar cookies with green food coloring earlier in the week. Just think about dunking a green cookie in a glass of green milk. Mmmmmm, it doesn't get better than that!

Whoa—a lot of bad things happen as a result of allowing jealousy and envy to creep into our lives, don't you think? Let me read you some verses from the Bible:

> A heart at peace gives life to the body,
>   but envy rots the bones. (Proverbs 14:30)

> Do not let your heart envy sinners,
>   but always be zealous for the fear of the
>   LORD. (Proverbs 23:17)

> Do not fret because of evil men
>   or be envious of the wicked,
> for the evil man has no future hope,
>   and the lamp of the wicked will be
>   snuffed out. (Proverbs 24:19-20)

> Anger is cruel and fury overwhelming,
>   but who can stand before jealousy?
>   (Proverbs 27:4)

> For where you have envy and selfish ambition, there you find disorder and every evil practice. (James 3:16)

The Bible is very clear about the danger of jealousy. It will twist and corrupt you inside. What's inside you will show itself eventually, and that can be disastrous.

Tie It Together

God wants us to focus on being content with what we have, with what He's given us. When we're jealous of someone else, it's like we're slapping God in the face. In essence, we're saying we're not satisfied with what He's given us. Does that make sense?

Pause here so they have time to process that thought. They may not have considered it before.

Imagine you bought a birthday present for someone. You really thought it out and spent some hard-earned cash. And then, when you went to the person's birthday party and gave him his present, he hardly showed any appreciation at all. In fact, he kept talking about the gifts he wished he had gotten. You wouldn't be too happy you were at that party, would you?

We're just reinforcing the point a little. You probably won't get much of a response here. Generally silence means agreement.

That's what we do to God when we wish we had someone else's looks, popularity, abilities or worldly "things." We can even be jealous of someone because of the boyfriend, girlfriend or parents he has.

The things we want but don't have can become our focus. When we concentrate on what God hasn't given us, we fail to see all that he has given us. We can easily become bitter. It's a trap. It can make us pursue the things in life that we don't have. That often leads to debt or going in a direction in life that God never intended for us. It's scary to think that jealousy can make us miss the road God has planned for us.

Can you tell me how you can keep envy or jealousy from taking root in your heart?

Give them a moment and see what they say here. Help them only if you need to. Being aware of jealousy is a first step. When they see that they're jealous or envious, they need to confess it to God and ask Him to help them get over it. Scripture is essential to this process. After you wrap it up in a minute, really encourage the kids to add the Scripture verses printed in the Working It into the Week section to their daily devotions.

In Dr. Seuss's children's book *Green Eggs and Ham*, the character resists and resists eating the green eggs and ham every time it's offered to him. Eventually he tries it and finds out he can handle it. He realizes that green eggs are not something to avoid, but something to embrace.

That's OK when it comes to green eggs, but allowing yourself to relax your guard and entertain jealous or envious thoughts is not OK. Being green with envy is anything but harmless. To believe it won't harm you is to fall for the devil's "green eggs and ham scam." Jealousy and envy are poison. Don't let them be part of your life.

Working It into the Week

Here are some verses for the kids this week.

Day 1: Proverbs 14:30

Day 2: Proverbs 23:17-19; 24:1-2

Day 3: Proverbs 24:19-20

Day 4: Proverbs 27:4

Day 5: James 3:13-16

Day 6: 1 Peter 2:1

The Missing Ingredient

What's the Point?

A life without love is as big a waste as chocolate chip cookies with a key ingredient left out.

Things You'll Need

- You'll need a recipe and all the ingredients necessary to make a batch of chocolate chip cookies, brownies or any other dessert your kids will really enjoy. We'll talk about chocolate chip cookies in this devotional, and if you need a good recipe, check out the back of a bag of Nestle's Toll House semi-sweet morsels. It's the recipe our kids (and their friends) love.

We'll be modifying the Nestle recipe by reducing the amount of sugar we put in the dough.

Here We Go

The plan is to make the cookies ahead of time with the help of at least one of the kids who will be in the family devotions.

Have your helper read aloud the list of ingredients from the back of the Nestle bag while you get them together on the table or counter. Next, have him read the mixing instructions to you step-by-step all the way through.

Here's the catch: You're going to leave out all of the white sugar and most of the brown. When your helper reads the part of the recipe that states, "Beat butter, granulated sugar, brown sugar and vanilla extract in large mixer bowl until creamy," you're going to modify the sugar part. You want him to know you're doing it, though. You might say something like this:

Let's hold off on adding the white sugar, and we'll use just one-quarter of a cup of the brown sugar. I don't think all that sugar is really necessary.

We'd like to leave all the sugar out, but a little brown sugar helps keep the color of the cookies looking more natural. Try to just keep going with the recipe. If your helper presses you about putting the sugar in, just pass it off with something like this:

I know the recipe calls for all that sugar, but I'm going to try it without it.

The key is to keep your answer short and sweet. You don't want a lot of questions yet. Now comes the hard part: You can't let the family sample the cookie dough from the bowl. You can't even let them snag a couple of warm cookies as they come out of the oven. Tell them they'll have to wait until you have your family devotions, and then they can have all they want (which won't be many without the sugar).

Before the family gets together for the devoes, pile the cookies on a plate. You may want to have some milk and glasses ready too. The kids will probably need it to wash the cookies down.

Get the family together and say something like this:

For devoes tonight I thought we'd let you have some fresh cookies as we talked. In fact, I'd like to get your opinion of this new chocolate chip cookie recipe.

As they chow down their first cookie, they'll discover these cookies don't taste as good as they look. I'd expect their appetites will disappear a lot quicker than the cookies will. Perfect. Now ask them a question or two.

So, how do you like them? On a scale of one to ten, one being terrible and ten being fantastic, how would you rate this recipe?

This is a good chance to see how polite and tactful your kids really are. If your kids are like mine, they'll tell you exactly what they think of the recipe, and it won't be anywhere near a ten. That's fine. Now tell them what you left out of the recipe.

The fact is, I only changed the recipe a little. I simply left most of the sugar out. I'm guessing by your reaction that the sugar was a pretty important ingredient.

Give them a moment for input here. They probably think leaving the sugar out was one step short of insanity. Sugar is a pretty important ingredient in a kid's diet. So far, so good. Now it's time to move on.

OK, normally I wouldn't dream of making cookies without most of the sugar in them. Nobody would. I think everybody knows that without sugar, cookies are pretty useless.

So why did I do it? I want you to remember that your life is kind of like a batch of cookies. If you leave a key ingredient out, your life isn't going to be nearly as good as it should be. Do you have any idea what this important ingredient is?

You're looking for feedback here. Hopefully you'll get a couple of guesses out of them. If they guess it right, great. If they're still stunned from the taste of the cookies, move on.

Let me read something to you from the Bible:

> And if I have a faith that can move mountains, but have not love, I am nothing. If I give all I possess to the poor and surrender my body to the flames, but have not love, I gain nothing." (1 Corinthians 13:2-3)

Tie It Together

If I'm making cookies, I can have the flour and the eggs, the chocolate chips and all the other ingredients mixed in perfectly. But if I leave out the sugar, I'm wasting my time. Cookies have to have sugar in them if they're going to be good.

In life, you can have a great education and do all kinds of good things. I could have everything this world has to offer, but according to God's Word, if I don't have love in the mix, I'm wasting my time. If I'm living without loving others, I'm not following God's recipe at all.

Now, God isn't talking about a "romantic" kind of love here. When He talks about love in the verses we just read, what's he talking about? Can you describe what this kind of love is like?

See what they have to say here, but don't linger too long on this part of the lesson. They'll get the idea, so you just want to make sure they understand some of the elements of love. Get whatever input they give you and then read First Corinthians 13:4-8 for a quick list.

Yup, love is patient, kind, humble and honest. It isn't rude, jealous or easily angered. It doesn't put itself first, but puts the needs and interests of others first instead. That's the kind of love that God wants you to add to your life.

If I don't add the sugar to the cookies, it won't jump in all by itself. It's the same with real love. Loving your family and others isn't necessarily something that happens all by itself. You have to work on being patient and kind. You have to ask God to help you put others ahead of yourself. If you don't work on it, the love that God describes in First Corinthians 13 simply won't exist in your life.

So, if you want a good cookie, don't forget the sugar. If you want a good life—one that is pleasing to God and others—don't forget the love. Love is the sugar of life.

Time to end. We don't want to go too long. If you try to cram too much teaching in, they'll get bored. One other thought, though. You may want to have a good batch of cookies (with all the sugar) made up ahead of time to pull out now. It always helps to end devoes with a good taste in their mouths.

Working It into the Week

The following are some verses you may want to jot down on a separate piece of paper for each of the kids. Encourage them to add this on to their own personal devotional time if they are doing that. If they aren't, here is a small place to start. These verses will help remind them about love throughout the week.

Day 1: 1 Corinthians 13:2-8

Day 2: Ephesians 4:2; 5:1-2

Day 3: 1 Timothy 4:12

Day 4: 2 Timothy 2:22

Day 5: 1 John 3:16-18

Day 6: Romans 12:9-10

It Serves You Right

What's the Point?

Real love doesn't delight in evil, but in real life often the opposite is the case. We'll contrast the two as soon as the kids calm down after your little milk "incident."

Things You'll Need

- You won't need much more than a glass of milk—and maybe nerves of steel. You can do this at a mealtime, or you can get the kids together for a little snack of milk and cookies or doughnuts.

  I chose milk because it's a normal thing to serve at mealtime for us and it washes out of clothes easily. You can do this activity with water if you'd prefer.

  This devotional really works best if there are a bunch of kids there to appreciate what you're doing. If you only have one child, consider having your child invite some friends over.

Here We Go

Let me lay out the plan for you here. The kids will be at the table for a meal or a snack. You'll be busy bringing things to the table. The last thing you'll bring is the milk. You're going to pour a glass of milk for each one. Now, if you don't normally do that, make an exception. Tell the kids you really want to serve them for this meal. They may sit back and gloat like kings. That'll do nicely.

As you bring over the last glass of milk, don't place it on the table, but pour it on your child's lap. This is the nerves-of-steel part. You normally wouldn't do such a thing (even though the thought may have crossed your mind once or twice). It goes against all those virtuous "parent" qualities you're supposed to display. That's what is going to make this a devotional that the kids will remember.

You'll have to target one of the kids to be your "receiver." Pick one that won't fly off the handle in anger. Think of something he's done recently that you weren't pleased about. That shouldn't be hard. Any little thing will work fine. Serve this person last. Try to get the others' attention before you do your little dairy dousing. You might say something like this:

You know, kids, "serving" is a pretty important thing. When I think of serving, I think of doing something nice for someone else. Not everybody thinks of it that way, though.

Get ready to pour the milk; you'll have all eyes on you after this next line. Be sure you're standing in a good position to get a clear shot at your chosen target's lap.

Now, take a look at this glass of milk for example.

Quickly dump it on the child's lap.

Some people look at serving as an opportunity to get even with someone. It's a "serves you right" kind of mentality.

The kids probably didn't hear your last line. They're in shock over what you just did. Keep your eyes open and watch the siblings for their reaction. Are they laughing? Are they happy their brother or sister got nailed with the milk? That will make the tie-in easier.

I'd expect the one you just soaked to blurt out something like, "What did you do that for?" Now is the time to remind him of the thing he did that was out of line. You want to say it matter-of-factly, without a trace of anger.

Remember when you (remind him of the incident)? Well, this is a little payback. It serves you right.

The shock of you making a statement like that should jolt the kids almost as much as when you emptied the glass on your kid's lap.

Now, you'll have to get the situation back under control here. I'd have the one with the milk all over him get changed while you clean up the floor. Tell him to hurry back so you can do a little explaining. You don't want the kids to think you've really flipped. As soon as the mess is cleaned up and your child has changed, you might say something like this:

Does anybody remember what I said as to why I poured the milk on (name)'s lap?

One of them will probably joyfully recount what you said. If not, remind them.

I think I said something about "it serves you right" for (the little incident you spoke of). Now, the real reason I did this was to help teach you an important lesson about love and life.

I noticed some of you seemed pretty happy at (the child's name with the milk on his lap)'s misfortune. That's a pretty natural reaction—most kids would react the same way.

The fact is, oftentimes we are secretly just a little bit happy when something goes wrong for someone we're supposed to care about. Let's take a look at a few familiar verses from the Bible:

> Love is patient, love is kind. It does not envy, it does not boast, it is not proud. It is not rude, it is not self-seeking, it is not easily angered, it keeps no record of wrongs. Love does not delight in evil but rejoices with the truth. It always protects, always trusts, always hopes, always perseveres. (1 Corinthians 13:4-7)

> Do not repay anyone evil for evil. Be careful to do what is right in the eyes of everybody. If it is possible, as far as it depends on you, live at peace with everyone. (Romans 12:17-18)

> Love must be sincere. Hate what is evil; cling to what is good. Be devoted to one another in brotherly love. Honor one another above yourselves. (Romans 12:9-10)

> Finally, all of you, live in harmony with one another; be sympathetic, love as brothers, be compassionate and humble. Do not repay evil with evil or insult with insult, but with blessing, because to this you were called so that you may inherit a blessing. For,

> "Whoever would love life
>   and see good days
> must keep his tongue from evil
>   and his lips from deceitful speech.

He must turn from evil and do good;
   he must seek peace and pursue it.
For the eyes of the Lord are on the righteous
   and his ears are attentive to their prayer,
but the face of the Lord is against
     those who do evil." (1 Peter 3:8-12)

I know, that was a lot of verses, but it was hard to eliminate any. Do what's best for your kids. It is more important to keep their attention, so if you have to eliminate some verses, go ahead. Let's move on.

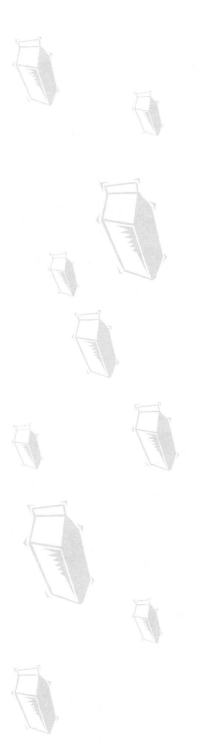

Tie It Together

It's very natural to be a little bit happy when something goes wrong for someone who has done something wrong to you. It's common to try to get someone back for something he says or does. The problem is that that is the world's way of doing things, not God's. God's way is very different. What are some of God's ways that are mentioned in the verses I just read?

Get a little feedback here, then key in on the most important elements.

We're supposed be peacemakers as much as we can. We're to live in harmony. We're to honor others as more important than ourselves. What does that mean?

Let them try to explain it, then build on what they give you.

Honoring others more than ourselves has to do with not being so wrapped up in how we're feeling or what another person did to hurt us. We need to give the benefit of the doubt to the other person and cut him some slack. We're supposed to be sympathetic to each other. We should be concerned about what is happening to the other person. When I dumped the milk on (child's name), you might have run to get a towel to help him dry himself off. That would have been sympathetic.

When we're insulted, what should we do? Do we come back with a real zinger and insult the other person right back?

Let them talk. Teenagers will probably come up with some wisecrack. That's OK. They're tracking with you, guaranteed. You need to wrap this up quickly so you don't keep repeating yourself and lose the kids' attention.

No, we're not supposed to try to get back at him. We're supposed to do good things to him. See, Christians are supposed to live and act differently from the rest of the world. A big part of that is how we treat others, especially when they don't treat us nicely.

If we aren't committed enough to God to love others this way, we have a spiritual problem, don't we? That passage in First Peter says that the Lord's face is against us if we do evil in return for evil done to us. It suggests that our actions will affect how God hears our prayers. That's a pretty good indication that this is important stuff to God, isn't it?

A little joking and teasing is great, but we need to be very careful about the things we say to each other. We need to be careful not to enjoy the moments when something goes wrong for someone we'd like to get even with in some way.

God wants us to "serve others right" in His terms, not our own. Serving others doesn't come naturally to us. It will take some real practice, but the payoff with God and with others is well worth it. Why don't we all agree that we'll work on this, OK?

Working It into the Week

Here are some references you can jot down on a piece of paper for each of the kids. Have them add these to their daily personal devotional times. These verses are packed with great stuff.

Day 1: 1 Corinthians 13:4-7

Day 2: Romans 12:9-11

Day 3: Romans 12:14

Day 4: Romans 12:17-21

Day 5: Galatians 6:10

Day 6: 1 Peter 3:8-12

Nip It in the Bud

What's the Point?

When we fail to be kind, we're messing with someone else's property—God's! We want the kids to realize that being unkind is really stepping over the bounds of love.

Things You'll Need

• Pick up a really nice bouquet of flowers or a flowering potted plant.

Make it the biggest bouquet you can reasonably afford. Ideally, get somebody else to buy the flowers for you. It would be nice if the person leading the devotions doesn't have to buy the flowers to give to himself (or herself). You may even want to buy the flowers for one of your kids if you have a girl. Be sure to put a floral gift card addressed to that person on it. Anyway, you'll want to arrange the flowers in a vase and put them on the kitchen table.

Now, if you have a traditional husband/wife family, Dad ought to buy the flowers for Mom and she can arrange them. This devotional will work fine with either Mom or Dad leading it.

We've written this devotional based on the bouquet and on the assumption that Mom has received the flowers from Dad and that Dad is the one who is leading the devotional. So, if you use the plant, or the receiver of the flowers is someone other than Mom, you'll have to adapt the dialogue a little bit.

Here We Go

Arrange to get the flowers a day in advance of the time you plan to have family devotions, if possible. Make a big deal in front of the kids about getting the flowers. You want to be sure that all the kids know you got them and that you really like them. At mealtime, add water and the vitamins that come with the bouquet to the vase or pot. You may even talk to the plant if you want to really ham it up. The whole idea is to be sure the kids get the impression that you <u>really</u> like the flowers.

The next part can work a couple of ways. At the start of family devotions you can pull out a pair of scissors and simply start clipping off all of the flowers. (If you don't get flowers very often, this is gonna hurt, but rest assured that it's for a good cause.) The kids will think you've gone nuts, but don't stop until all the flowers are cut off.

A more powerful option is to have your oldest child do the cutting. This would get the point across really well, so we'd encourage you to do it. Sometimes it's good to get the kids involved like this. If you opt to do it this way, talk to your eldest privately about it just before devoes time. Then get the kids together and have them sit around the table that has the flowers on it.

Make an excuse to leave the room for a moment. That will be your son's or daughter's cue to start clipping away at the flowers while you're gone and the other kids are there watching. The other kids' shock will be even greater if they see one of their brothers or sisters doing the cutting.

The kids will be expecting a reaction when you walk in and see a vase full of stems and the flowers lying on the table. They'll be pretty disappointed to find out their older sibling isn't in trouble. Now you'll need to start making some sense of all this. In this devotional, we went with the assumption that you had your oldest child do the clipping, so if you did otherwise, just adjust the wording accordingly. You might start out by saying something like this:

What a crazy thing to do, huh? Here's a great-looking bouquet of flowers that have been ruined. Did the flowers get clipped by the person who owned them?

This seems like an obvious answer, but ask the question anyway—we want to establish this point in their minds. We'll build on it later.

No, the one who did the cutting of the flowers wasn't the one who owned them. This kind of action would normally be considered an awfully unkind thing to do. What potential might this plant have had?

If you need to rephrase the question, fine. Try something like, "What are some of the good things we might have gotten from this plant if its flowers hadn't been cut off?" You're looking for responses like: It would have looked nice, it would have smelled good, it would have made Mom happy, etc.

What are the flowers good for now?

They'll probably say the flowers are good for nothing and that they should be thrown in the garbage.

Yeah, you're right. The flowers had the potential to look good, make the kitchen more cheery, add a nice smell and make Mom happy just having them around. Now they're not much good for any of that.

Now let me read some Bible verses to you:

Be kind and compassionate to one another, forgiving each other, just as in Christ God forgave you. (Ephesians 4:32)

Make sure that nobody pays back wrong for wrong, but always try to be kind to each other and to everyone else. (1 Thessalonians 5:15)

A kind man benefits himself,
    but a cruel man brings trouble on himself.
(Proverbs 11:17)

Tie It Together

A lot of care went into arranging those flowers in a vase and making sure they had all of the water and nutrients they needed. After all that, it was pretty crazy to cut the flowers off, wasn't it?

Now, imagine that it was a tree instead of a bunch of flowers. Imagine I planted that tree years ago and watered it regularly so it wouldn't dry up. In the winter I brushed the heavy snow off of it so it wouldn't bend over and snap. I watched its growth with pride. How do you think I'd feel if someone who didn't even own it starting hacking limbs off of it for no good reason?

Give them a moment to process this. The answer is obvious, but they may still be trying to figure out what your point is.

I'd be pretty upset. I think any of us would be. Someone shouldn't damage something that doesn't belong to him, right?

OK, this was a key question. You're leading them right where you want them. They have to agree with you on this point. As soon as they do, move on.

How do you think God feels when we're unkind to other people, like when we carelessly cut them down with an unkind comment or chop them down to size with a sarcastic remark?

You've dropped the bomb on them. If they weren't sure where you were heading before, they are now. You may get an answer out of them at this point, or they may be quiet as clams. Either way is all right. Keep going.

God "owns" all of us, doesn't He? He created us, nurtured us, protected us, watched us grow. Taking all that into account, did you ever think that when we do or say unkind things to each other, we're also offending God? In God's eyes, what right do we have to be unkind to someone else, to one of His children?

See what they say here. The answer is pretty obvious: They have no right.

You got it: In God's eyes we don't have the right to be unkind to other people. He asks us to love each other, and an important part of showing that love is being kind to each other. And that's true even when we don't feel like being kind and even when the other person hasn't exactly been kind to us.

Hold up a clipped flower.

See, when we're unkind to others, even brothers or sisters, we may be undoing some of the things God is trying to do in their lives. If someone gets hurt enough, he may have trouble ever reaching the potential God designed for him.

The verses we read a few minutes ago stressed being kind to others no matter how we feel we were treated. If you feel you've been wronged, you may need to forgive the person who did it to you. Don't give in to the temptation to be unkind back. Nip that kind of response in the bud. The verse we read in Proverbs says we'll benefit if we react with kindness. That's a good thing. We all fail in this area, but let's keep working on it, OK?

By this point they have gotten the message. Let's leave it alone for now. If the subject comes up again, by all means bring up another discussion, but you don't want to overload them right now.

Working It into the Week

I'd encourage you to jot these verses down on a piece of paper for each of them to review in their daily personal devotions. You may also want to leave the vase with the stems poking out of it on the table for a couple of days as a visual reminder of the lesson.

Day 1: 1 Corinthians 13:4-8

Day 2: Colossians 3:12-14

Day 3: Galatians 5:22-26

Day 4: Ephesians 4:32

Day 5: 1 Thessalonians 5:15

Day 6: Proverbs 11:17

The Devil's Trap

What's the Point?

Real love requires trust, and we want to encourage the kids to trust God and His plan for sex.

Preface

We'll be hitting a couple of sensitive topics during this devotional—namely, premarital sex and pornography. Wait! Before you start flipping the pages to get to the next devotional as quickly as you can, take into consideration the fact that children today are learning about sex from a lot of unsavory sources. So, wouldn't you rather discuss these topics now, before your kids hear about them from something or someone that is less than appropriate?

If you feel the kids are too young for this one, save it for a later date. Having said that, however, be sure your kids really are too young before you let this slide by. Each child is different, so you'll want to take each kid's personality and maturity into consideration before you do this devotional. Remember, though, that junior-high-aged kids are more than old enough for this discussion. If you have a mix of younger and older kids, you may want to split them up and do something different with the kids you deem too young for this devotional.

I know the topic is awkward to deal with, but don't avoid it. You'll be glad you did, and your kids will be better off because of it.

Here We Go

You'll probably want to do this around the kitchen table at home. I did it at a restaurant, and it was probably a little discomforting for other people eating to see the rat trap. If you have some kids who are still too young for this, do the devoes after they're in bed.

Keep the traps in a bag out of sight for starters. Light the candle and get the kids together. You might start out with something like this:

See this flame here? It's one of God's amazing creations. Tell me some good things that fire can do.

We're just getting their brains in gear here. They should come up with things like: It keeps us warm, it gives us heat and hot water, it can give us light, it can sterilize a needle, it can bring healing, comfort and protection and it can cook our food. You get the idea.

Yeah, a lot of good things can come from a fire. What are some of the bad things that can result from a flame?

Again, get their input. It can burn, scar, bring unbearable pain and destroy.

So God made fire, and it has tremendous potential for either good or bad, depending on how you use it, right?

You may get a nod here. Don't worry if you don't get a response; they're tracking with you. Take it to the next level.

There are other things God made that in a similar way can be really good or really bad, depending on how they're used. The devil is well aware of this, and he's an expert in taking good things that God made and twisting them for a bad use.

Pull out the <u>mouse trap</u> and let the kids see it. Keep the rat trap hidden from their view.

Take our mouths, for example. They are capable of great good, like when we encourage someone. Our mouths can also do real damage, like when we tear someone down. The devil can use a good thing that God created—our mouths—as a trap. The devil wants you to use the mouth God made and gave you to say things that are wrong or hurtful. Can you think of any other examples of good things that the devil can use as a trap?

Don't worry if they don't respond here. They're thinking. If they say "sex," I'd be surprised, but it will open the door nicely for you. I'll assume you'll have to bring it up.

There is another thing God made that is very good, but the devil loves to trap people with it when they use it the wrong way. The devil has made this one of his most effective traps. Any idea what I'm talking about?

This is only a pause. If they're thinking "sex," they'll probably wait until you bring it up. Keep moving, there's no turning back now.

Sex. Something God created for great good in a marriage setting. Something the devil uses as a trap for horrible destruction outside of marriage. The devil is always setting traps for us, (hold up the **mouse trap)**, like this mouse trap. Sex is one of his biggest traps.

Pull out the <u>rat trap</u> and let them look at it for a moment.

Yeah, sex is one of Satan's big-league traps. Let's take a look at it. Here on the bait pedal are sex and pornography. He wants you to nibble on them. I wrote some of the devil's lies about it around the trap. Let's take a look at them.

Things You'll Need

- Pick up a mouse trap and a rat trap from the hardware store. You'll want to get the traditional, spring-loaded type. If you haven't seen a rat trap like this, let me tell you, it's a nasty-looking thing.

- You'll also need a candle and some matches, and maybe a pencil to use to set off the trap.

- Next, you'll need to use a fine-point marker to write some things on the rat trap. The one I bought had writing all over it, so I used some white latex paint to cover over what was written there. You don't have to get complete coverage. In fact, being able to read the words *rat trap* through the paint covering is a good thing.

After the paint is dry, write the words sex *and* pornography *on a small piece of paper and wedge or tape it onto the bait pedal. Then write the words and phrases listed below all over the top wood surface of the trap. As you write, leave room below each phrase for you to write another short sentence during the actual devotional time. Here's the list for you to write in advance:*

- Satisfaction guaranteed!

- Safe!

- Feels great!

- You can handle it!

- Be free!

- You'll be glad you did!

- Thrills! Excitement!

- This is living!

- None of the kids I know who are sexually active or who watch porn seems to experience any bad effects!

- Nobody will ever know!

This part is long. Normally I wouldn't talk so long without breaking for input. Play it by ear. I marched right through it because I didn't want to break the momentum. You can ask them things like, "Does this make sense?" occasionally. You'll probably get a nod. Take that as your cue to keep moving.

Satisfaction guaranteed! Really? The truth is, sex outside of marriage can lead to terrible regrets. (Write the word <u>regrets</u> below "Satisfaction guaranteed!")

Safe! On the contrary, there is no such thing as "safe sex" outside of marriage, no matter what you've heard. Sperm can penetrate the condom. And what about disease? Condom manufacturers don't guarantee a thing. In fact, they have a set of instructions for "proper" condom use that are ridiculous. Nobody in the heat of passion is going to follow their procedures. There is no safe sex. (Write the word <u>deadly</u> below the word "Safe!")

Feels great! Sex does feel great, but when you engage in it outside of God's plan, before you're married, the great feeling is going to come with some real pain. I'm talking about emotional pain. When a couple breaks up and they've had sex, the pain is much more intense. It's the feeling that you gave all you had to that other person, but it wasn't enough. You simply weren't good enough. (Write the word <u>pain</u> below "Feels great!")

You can handle it! Not a chance. Sex is too big, too powerful. This is also true of pornography. It is much more powerful than you can dream. It slowly digs its roots into you and you can't pull it out. You need to avoid it—the videos, cable, the Internet—in all of its forms. It will absolutely cripple you. (Write the word <u>crippling</u> below "You can handle it!")

Be free! That's a joke. Sex before marriage is enslaving. Pornography absolutely enslaves and won't let you go. (Write the word <u>enslaves</u> below "Be free!")

You'll be glad you did! Wrong. You'll be plagued by guilt. (Write the word <u>guilt</u> below "You'll be glad you did!")

Thrills! Excitement! Oh, yeah, there can be thrills, all right. Sex can be really exciting at the time, but that doesn't last. You're left with a lot of hurt if you have sex outside of marriage. (Write the word <u>hurt</u> below "Thrills! Excitement!")

This is living! No, this is dying. Sex, whether you're actively involved in it or you're using pornography, kills. It kills your future and your chances for great sex in the context of marriage someday. And, sex can literally kill you if you contract a sexually transmitted disease. (Write the word <u>kills</u> below "This is living!")

None of the kids I know who are sexually active or who watch porn seems to experience any bad effects! *Yet.* That's the key word: *yet.* The damage may not show for years. It may not show until they're married and the porn won't let go of them. You don't know the emotional agony they may be going through now, and you can't imagine what it might be like later. These kids are caught in a trap and they don't know it. They're poisoning themselves and think they're immune to the deadly effects just because the symptoms haven't shown themselves yet. (Write the word <u>yet</u> below "None of the kids I know who are sexually active or who watch porn seems to experience any bad effects!")

Nobody will ever know! Ah yes, the old line that has suckered more people into the trap than anything else. The fact is, you *will* be found out. God knows immediately, and His Word guarantees that your sins will find you out. Hiding something from your parents is one thing, but from God? Get real. (Write the phrase "You will be found out" below "Nobody will ever know!")

Does this make sense to you?

Give them a chance to respond, but I'd guess they'll be pretty quiet. It's a heavy topic. Don't get nervous. You're getting through.

Tie It Together

First Corinthians 13:7 tells us that true love "trusts." If we really love God, if we claim to be Christians, then we need to trust Him. We need to trust Him enough to do it His way, even if we're tempted to believe the devil's lies regarding sex and pornography. Does that make sense?

Let's see if they'll give us a little input here. We just made a key point. Avoiding sexual sin has a lot to do with our love for God and trusting Him. If you don't get input, move on.

God wants us to avoid the trap. Sex is a great thing, but only when used as it was designed. We need to delay areas of sexual gratification and trust God that He will make it worth the wait later.

You must do it God's way, even if nobody else does it right. Listen to these verses:

> Don't let anyone look down on you because you are young, but set an example for the believers in speech, in life, in love, in faith and in purity. (1 Timothy 4:12)

> Flee the evil desires of youth, and pursue righteousness, faith, love and peace, along with those who call on the Lord out of a pure heart. (2 Timothy 2:22)

> Flee from sexual immorality. All other sins a man commits are outside his body, but he who sins sexually sins against his own body. Do you not know that your body is a temple of the Holy Spirit, who is in you, whom you have received from God? You are not your own; you were bought at a price. Therefore honor God with your body. (1 Corinthians 6:18-20)

The devil will try to deceive you into buying into his lies about sex. I want God's best for you. God invented sex and He knows how it will work best. Real love trusts. Trust God that His way is the best. Avoid the devil's traps. Do it God's way, OK?

If you haven't demonstrated the trap yet, now is the time to do it. Carefully set the trap and use a pencil to trip it. The power will probably break the pencil. That's good.

Leave the trap out for a few days or hang it on the fridge as a reminder of this lesson.

Working It into the Week

You may want to give them some verses to add to their daily personal devotional times during the week. Below are some suggestions:

Day 1: 1 Timothy 4:12

Day 2: 2 Timothy 2:22

Day 3: 1 Corinthians 6:18-20

Day 4: Ecclesiastes 3:1, 5

Day 5: Proverbs 5:1-14; 7:24-27

Day 6: Proverbs 5:21-23

Body Shop

What's the Point?

We usually think of forgiveness as something nice we're supposed to do for someone else (who probably doesn't deserve it). We'll show that forgiveness is vital for our well-being too.

Things You'll Need

- You'll need to locate a local auto body shop, a place where you bring a car to get its body looking like new after an accident. If you don't know where a shop like this is, try looking in the yellow pages under the heading of "auto body and fender work." Most auto dealerships have a body shop in the back too. This will probably be your best bet.

- You'll also need a camera to take a few pictures. A disposable camera would work great for this. You can pick one up for under $10.

- Before doing this devotional, you'll need to talk to the body shop manager. Explain to him that you're trying to teach your kids the value of forgiveness and that you'd like to show them before and after examples of body work on a car to illustrate the point. You might also want to tell him that the more banged up the car is, the better, because it will help you illustrate your point.

Here We Go

You may want to start the devotions by grabbing the "before" and "after" pictures, piling the kids into the car and then driving to the body shop. You don't need to go inside; you could just drive through the lot and see if there are a couple of damaged cars there waiting for body work. Be sure to point them out to the kids.

Next, drive to a fast-food place and get everyone something to snack on. When they're all at the table, pull out the "before" pictures. You might say something like this:

A couple of weeks ago I was talking to the manager of the body shop we just went to. He sent me these pictures. Take a look at them.

Show them the "before" pictures only. They should see the damage to the car easily.

What do you think happened here? Whose fault do you think the accident was?

If they don't know the answer, that's OK. You're just trying to get them thinking.

Well, even if the accident wasn't this car owner's fault, his car sure is messed up.

Pull out the "after" pictures of the car.

I have some other pictures here too. Here's the very same car after they did the body work on it. How does it look now?

Let them see the difference. They should say it looks pretty good. That's fine. Let's keep rolling. We need to make some sense of all of this.

Tie It Together

OK, so we've seen the car with the scrapes and dents, and we've seen it looking like new after the body shop worked on it. Let me ask you a stupid question: If you were given that car as a gift, how would you rather have it, with or without the dents?

Now, you know the answer to the question, but the kids may try giving you a hard time and say they like it better with the dents. Don't worry about it. They're just trying to yank your chain a little. Just move on.

Of course we'd rather have the car without the dents. The dents take away from the looks and value of the car. Can you imagine someone insisting on keeping the dents in his car just so everyone he met would feel sorry for him, or so others would know how much of a jerk the other driver was? Can you imagine a person refusing to get the body work done even if it wouldn't cost him anything?

Give them a moment to think about this. They may not say anything, but you're going to build on this thought in a minute. You want them to process this and come to the conclusion that it would be foolish to leave the dents in for those reasons.

Did you find it amazing how the body shop was able to make a car with that much damage look so good in the end?

This is another important point. Remember, the more damage the car had initially, the better.

Let me read you some verses from the Bible:

> For if you forgive men when they sin against you, your heavenly Father will also forgive you. But if you do not forgive men

Ask if you can send him a single-use camera to take some pictures of a nicely smacked up car before and after they do the body work. Tell him you'll enclose either postage or money so that he can return the camera to you. This should be a pretty simple request, so hopefully the manager will agree to do it. If not, call another body shop.

Now, if you'd rather, you could see if the manager would let you bring the kids to see a car they haven't worked on yet. You could take the "before" pictures yourself and leave the single-use camera with him to take the "after" pictures when they're through with the work.

If you do take the kids to the body shop, don't explain anything to them yet. The time for that will be later, after the car is fixed up and you have pictures to show. Be sure to leave the manager postage or some money so that he can return the camera to you. It would be more fun for the kids to do it this way, but you'll have a harder time getting permission from a body shop to do it.

When you get the camera back, get your film processed. Did you get good "before" and "after" shots? If you did, you're ready to go.

Note: If you have difficulty finding a body shop that will take the photos for you, you can probably find "before" and "after" car crash images on the Internet that you could print out.

We're going to assume you did the whole picture thing through the mail for the purposes of how we're writing this.

their sins, your Father will not forgive your sins. (Matthew 6:14-15)

Then Peter came to Jesus and asked, "Lord, how many times shall I forgive my brother when he sins against me? Up to seven times?"

Jesus answered, "I tell you, not seven times, but seventy-seven times." (Matthew 18:21-22)

Bear with each other and forgive whatever grievances you may have against one another. Forgive as the Lord forgave you. (Colossians 3:13)

Above all, love each other deeply, because love covers over a multitude of sins. (1 Peter 4:8)

I showed you the pictures of the car before and after the work was done by the body shop to illustrate forgiveness to you. Just like the car was all banged up, we can get "banged up" too. Somebody might deliberately hurt us, or it may be an accident. The person who hurts us may not even be aware that he is doing so.

When the damage is done, we have a decision to make: We can forgive the person and work to shed the hurt and damage, or we can hold a grudge. If we choose to hold a grudge, we can be sure it will show, just like we would be able to see the scrapes and dents if we were driving the damaged car around.

A damaged car, with paint scraped off of it and bare metal exposed, will quickly rust. In the same way, if we don't forgive others, it will lead to a type of corrosion in us too. That corrosion is called bitterness.

If someone doesn't have his car fixed and drives around with it all smashed up, it can be a reflection on the person driving the car. In the same way, if we choose not to forgive someone so that people see how we were wronged, we're the ones who lose. Forgiveness isn't just for the benefit of the one who wronged us. It's a gift to ourselves. Does this make sense to you?

Stop now and get some input before you go too long and get "preachy." Believe me, the kids understand exactly what you're trying to get across. You should wrap it up, pronto. Pull out the "before" and "after" pictures of the car again.

When you look at the "before" and "after" pictures of the car, there's no comparison. If I had a choice, I'd want to be driving the car that has had the body work done, wouldn't you?

That's what God wants for us. He knows that when we fail to forgive someone, no matter how right we were and how wrong the other person was, we are only hurting ourselves. We're like the person driving around in a damaged car. When a car has been banged up, it needs to be fixed. When we've been wronged somehow, we need to get fixed too. Forgiving those who wronged us is how we do it.

There's one other thing that we need to remember: Body work on a car isn't cheap.

If you know the cost of the body work on the car you saw, this would be a good time to mention it.

Body work can take a lot of time and effort if the damage is extensive. In the same way, forgiveness takes some deliberate effort too. It's an important element of learning to be a loving person. Why don't we all agree that we'll work on forgiveness, OK?

You may only get a nod here, but that's enough. Put "before" and "after" pictures of the damaged car up on the refrigerator as a reminder to everyone. Oh, and you may want to think about someone you need to forgive. Start doing the "body work" on that one and don't be afraid to share it with the kids. They need to see how the Bible is relevant to you too.

Working It into the Week

Here are some verses to help remind the kids (and you) about forgiveness this week. Jot them down for each of the kids. You might want to jot it on the back of one of the smashed-car photos for a good visual reminder.

Day 1: Matthew 6:9-15

Day 2: Matthew 18:21-35

Day 3: Mark 11:25

Day 4: Luke 6:35-37

Day 5: Colossians 3:12-14

Day 6: 1 Peter 4:8

Gagging Your Bragging

What's the Point?

First Corinthians 13:4 tells us that genuine love doesn't boast. Unfortunately, most people love to brag. A little role-playing will help remind the kids that bragging is wrong (and that it's pretty ugly too!).

Things You'll Need

- Photocopies of the role-playing scripts for each kid.

You'll be doing a little role-playing for this devotional. There are two short skits included in this text. Pick the one you think will work best with the kids. Both scripts are written to have only two characters in it. If you only have one child, you can take one of the parts. If you have more than two children, you may want to do both scripts just so that no one feels left out. Make a photocopy of the script(s) on pages 60–63 in advance for each kid who will have a part in the skit.

These skits should be a very non-threatening way to role-play. The kids are handed a script and assigned a part, and then they simply read their parts out loud.

Here We Go

OK, before you get everyone together for devoes, make sure that you look at the two skits and decide which one works best for the kids. Both of them are pretty obvious. One character will be "normal" and the other will be a real egomaniac. When you're assigning parts, keep that in mind. If you're taking a part, you may want to be the big bragger. It will be easier to pick the person in the skit apart later if it isn't your child. Also, you may want to change the gender of the characters depending on the kids you'll have in the devoes.

The first skit is titled "The Interview" and the second is "New Neighbor." Remember to coach the characters to use some real enthusiasm.

After you're done with the skit(s), say something like this:

OK, so the bragging was a little exaggerated here, but I think you get the idea. Bragging isn't very pretty, is it?

Get their input here. You may only get a shake of the head. That's fine.

God can't stand bragging. Why do you suppose He feels that way?

Hopefully they'll start thinking here. Any answer they give will probably work. You'll narrow things down for them after you get some feedback.

If I'm bragging, it puts the spotlight on me. It's a way of getting attention for myself and putting myself above others. When I brag, I'm taking credit for something that would have been impossible without God. No wonder God doesn't like bragging. Listen to some verses from the Bible:

Therefore, as it is written: "Let him who boasts boast in the Lord." (1 Corinthians 1:31)

Do nothing out of selfish ambition or vain conceit, but in humility consider others better than yourselves. (Philippians 2:3)

May I never boast except in the cross of our Lord Jesus Christ. (Galatians 6:14)

"Let not the wise man boast of his wisdom
    or the strong man boast of his strength
    or the rich man boast of his riches,
but let him who boasts boast about this:
    that he understands and knows me,
that I am the LORD, who exercises kindness,
    justice and righteousness on earth,
    for in these I delight," declares the LORD.
                                        (Jeremiah 9:23-24)

Do not boast about tomorrow,
    for you do not know what a day
        may bring forth. (Proverbs 27:1)

What are these verses saying?

A little input here is good. Take anything they give you and sum it up for them.

Tie It Together

God doesn't want us to brag. He wants us to think of others first and not put the spotlight on ourselves.

The story of David and Goliath in First Samuel 17 is a great example of this concept. Goliath is the big bragger. He challenges any person in the whole Israelite army to come out and fight him.

He's really saying he's a better warrior than anyone in the king's entire army. He tells David that he's going to rip him apart and feed him to the birds and the wild animals. He's a classic example of a bragger.

David brags too, but his bragging is different. He brags about God and how God will help him defeat Goliath. He gives the credit to God. If we want to brag, that's the way to do it.

God wanted Goliath to be cut down to size a bit. He had a big head, and I guess God decided it ought to come off. That's exactly what happened. After David took Goliath down with a slingshot, he grabbed Goliath's own sword and lopped the giant's big head off.

Bad bragging talks about how great I am. Good bragging talks about how great God is. Do you understand the difference?

That was a very important point. We should only brag about God and what He does or what He allows us to do. The key is to give God credit for the good things we do.

We should brag about God. After all, where would we be without Him? He gives us our health, our strength and our minds so we can do things. To brag about ourselves is to take credit for something God has done.

Have you ever done something good and then somebody else took credit for it? It isn't right, and something like that can really get us upset, right? Well, when we brag about something we did, we're doing the same thing to God: We're stealing credit from Him, who gave us our abilities in the first place.

There's a fine line between bragging and simply being excited about what we said or did that we're happy about. The difference is where the credit goes. If you keep the credit, it's bragging.

Can you give me examples of things you hear others brag about?

You're trying to really bring this home to them. They need to think about how other kids brag, and even how they themselves brag. This awareness is the first step toward stopping it in their own lives. Take whatever input they give and wrap it up.

Let's work on this, OK? Let's try not to put ourselves ahead of others or get the spotlight on ourselves, but try to get it on God. Let's give credit where credit is due and try to start gagging our bragging!

Working It into the Week

Here are some verses for the kids to add to their daily personal devotional times this week. Jot the references down on a separate sheet of paper for each of them.

Day 1: Psalm 34:2; 44:8; Proverbs 27:1-2

Day 2: Jeremiah 9:23-24; Galatians 6:14

Day 3: 1 Corinthians 1:26-31

Day 4: 2 Corinthians 12:6; Ephesians 2:8-10

Day 5: Philippians 2:3-4

Day 6: 1 Samuel 17

Skit #1: The Interview

Setting:

The scene is set in the personnel manager's office at a large corporation. (A kitchen table will work fine as the desk.)

As the scene opens, the personnel manager is sitting at the desk or table, shuffling papers.

Cast of Characters:

CJ: High school student, interviewing for her first job.

MR. BLABBER: Personnel manager of a large corporation.

Action:

CJ ENTERS and stands uneasily in front of MR. BLABBER's desk.

MR. BLABBER: (Looking up from papers and smiling) You must be CJ, and you're here for an employment interview, right?

CJ: (A bit nervously) Uh, yeah.

MR. BLABBER: (Pointing toward a chair) Take a seat. Is this your first job interview?

CJ: (Nodding) Uh-huh.

MR. BLABBER: (Confident) I knew it. The moment you stepped up to my desk I said to myself, "This kid's a rookie, I'll bet it's her first job." And I was right, wasn't I? You bet I was right. I'm always right when it comes to stuff like that. If you get the job you'll soon learn I have an uncanny ability to "read" people. (Looking at the paper on his desk) It says here you'll be turning sixteen soon. I'm guessing you don't have your driver's license yet, am I right?

CJ: Well, no, like you said, I'm not even sixteen yet. I can't legally drive.

MR. BLABBER: (Nodding) I could "read" that on you. I'm guessing somebody drove you here, right?

CJ: Yeah, my mom.

MR. BLABBER: (Proud of himself) See? I'm right again, right I am! I'm telling you, I can "read" people. It's almost spooky. (Leaning back and pausing for a moment)

I remember my first job. The company interviewed twenty-seven applicants, and you know who they hired?

CJ: Let me take a wild guess, I'm going to say . . .

MR. BLABBER: (Interrupting) Me. They hired me. Out of twenty-seven applicants they hired me. And they were glad they did, let me tell you. Oh yeah, they were real glad. Within three months I was top salesman. Three months! I was selling more than veteran salesmen twice my age. After I left the company for a better offer, they were really hurting without me. They went belly-up within a year. By that time I was already climbing the ladder at the new job I was at. They made me regional sales manager within two years of hiring me. That was a real record in their history books. They had never seen anyone sell like I did. It wasn't long before I was the national sales manager with a big office and an even bigger paycheck. What do you think about that?

CJ: Sounds like you've been pretty lucky.

MR. BLABBER: Lucky? No, it was hard work that got me where I am today. I earned every bit of it. You know what kind of car I drive?

CJ: (Bored but trying not to act like it) I don't know. A Ford maybe?

MR. BLABBER: (Shaking his head) Hardly. You won't believe how much I paid for my cars. Neither of them is a Ford. On your way out, look for my parking space in the lot. It has my name on it. My spot is right next to the CEO of the company, or as I like to say it, his parking spot is right next to mine! (Glancing at watch) Wow, look at the time! I'll have to run. We'll review your application and let you know if you get the job.

CJ: (Surprised) That's it? Don't you want to ask me some questions or something?

MR. BLABBER: (Looking at papers on desk) No, I think I have everything I need here. We covered the important issues, and I've given you something more important than a simple interview today. I've given you the inspiration of my successes to light the way for you. If you can do half as well as I have, you'll really turn some heads.

CJ: (Stands to leave) Well, thank you for the, ah, interview. I hope I'll be able to work for you.

MR. BLABBER: (Standing and nodding head) That's the spirit. Aim high!

MR. BLABBER motions to the door. CJ turns and EXITS.

Skit #2: New Neighbor

Setting:

The scene is set at the front door of a new neighbor's home. As the scene opens, MEG walks up the steps and rings the doorbell.

Cast of Characters:

MEG: Girl living next door to the new neighbor. She has lived in the area all her life.

STEPHEN: The new neighbor, very proud, "stuck up."

Action:

STEPHEN: (Opening the door) Hello.

MEG: (Smiling) Hi, I'm Meg, your next-door neighbor. I saw the moving truck this morning and thought I'd stop by to welcome you to the neighborhood.

STEPHEN: Oh, hi. (Scanning the neighborhood with a doubtful look) I'm not so sure how long I'll be your neighbor, though. My dad got a transfer. We had to move quickly. That's how we ended up in this dump. We'll be moving to something much nicer soon, believe me. How can you stand living in an area like this?

MEG: (A little surprised at his reaction, she sounds a little unsure) I'm not sure what you mean. I, I like this neighborhood.

STEPHEN: (Certain she must be joking) Right. I'm sure you do. Who wouldn't want to live in a little house with no pool and a garage that can hardly fit two cars in it? I'm not even going to unpack my boxes. I wouldn't get half of my clothes in the dinky little closet in my room. And then there are the trophies.

MEG: The trophies?

STEPHEN: (Shrugs) Yeah, tons of them. I'm a natural athlete, and not in just one sport either. I'm all around. I'll probably be in the Olympics someday. My last coach was sorry to see me move, let me tell you. The team doesn't have a chance at the championship without me.

MEG: (A little sarcastically) Wow, you're a regular wonder. I guess I'm pretty lucky to have you living next door to me, even if it's only until you find a nicer place.

STEPHEN: (Doesn't see her sarcasm) Yeah, I guess you could say that. Your girl-friends at school will think you're the luckiest kid around. They'll want to come over to your house all the time.

MEG: Just so they can be closer to you, is that it?

STEPHEN: (Grins and nods) You got that right, girl. The women are always hanging on me. That's what happens when you're smart, athletic and handsome like I am. Wait until you see my car. Oh yeah, the girls will come running.

MEG: (She's heard enough) Well, hey, I'd better get going. If any of my friends sees me talking to you they'll get really jealous and probably won't speak to me for the rest of the year. Besides, I should clear out of the doorway and give some of the other girls a chance to meet you.

MEG turns and leaves.

STEPHEN: (Calling after her) I can't remember your name, but thanks for stopping by. Feel free to come by again after I've had a chance to unpack a little. I can show you some of my trophies.

Sooner or Later

What's the Point?

There are two kinds of patience. One type is simply being patient with others in our day-to-day lives. We cover that type in the "Shop 'til Their Drop" devotional in this book (see page 133). The other type of patience is when we have to wait, sometimes for years, for God's timing on something. Some call it "delayed gratification"; we call it plain tough! We'll use the kids' choices about the snack as a launching ramp to talk about delayed gratification.

Things You'll Need

- Pick up a favorite candy bar and a bottle of soda or juice for each of the kids. Make sure the soda or juice is ice cold when it comes to devotional time. Get the candy bar in the biggest size you can.

- While you're at the grocery store, see if they offer gift certificates. If they do, pick one up for each of the kids using your grocery money. Don't worry—if your kids are at all like mine, you won't really have to give the certificate away. You'll probably still be able to use the certificates the next time you go grocery shopping. The certificate will make a great visual, though.

If money is tight, just pick up one certificate or make your own "I Owe You" certificate. Then you don't have to lay out any cash now. Make the amount for $10 or $20. We'll explain more about this later.

You want to offer the candy and soda at a time when the kids are hungry and thirsty. You can do the devoes later. Maybe you can

Here We Go

When the kids are nice and hungry or thirsty, get them together or catch them individually and say something like this:

Hey, you look hungry. I have a little snack for you to hold you over until dinner is ready, but I also have a deal for you.

Just the sight of that ice-cold soda or juice is probably making them a little impatient. Tell them about your deal.

Here's the deal: You can have this soda and candy now, or any time up until dinner, but if you wait and don't have either of them, I'll give you a reward.

A reward? Depending on the age of your kids, they may look at you like, "You've got to be kidding." Anyway, they'll want to hear the details of it.

If you can wait, and you don't take these, I'll promise to give you a chance someday, maybe a few months or so from now, to spend $20 at the grocery store to buy all the candy and soda you want. What do you think?

You need to make sure they understand that you aren't giving them the $20 now. Don't let them pin you down to a date when you'll give it either. Be vague. It won't be for at least several months.

I'd be surprised if they didn't grab the candy bars and soda or juice and run. If they do, great. If they don't, you'll switch gears a little as you do the rest of this devotional. You'll be able to tell them that they made a wise choice, and they need to do it in other, more important areas of life. Then go on with the devoes.

I'm going to go way out on a limb and figure that your child is wiping chocolate off of his chin already. You're done for now.

When you're ready to actually finish the devoes, get the kids together and say something like this:

Do you remember when I offered you the candy and soda, and I offered a reward not to take it? What was the reward? Do you remember?

They should remember some of the details. That's fine. After they tell you, move on.

Now, there aren't many kids who would have resisted the cold soda and candy in exchange for a promise that someday they'd get a $20 snack spree at the grocery store. Did any of you deep down doubt that you'd ever get the snack spree? I mean, did you think that I'd just forget all about it and you'd lose out completely?

I'll bet that's exactly what they were thinking. OK, now it's time to whip out the grocery store certificates or IOUs that they lost out on.

Well, the fact is, I was serious about that promise, and just to prove it to you, here are the gift certificates I purchased from the store for any of you who might have decided to take me up on my deal. The certificates would have been yours to use when we went to the grocery store sometime.

I'd imagine there will be some complaining right about now. You'll probably hear, "But you never said you had certificates. That wasn't fair!" or something along those lines. If you have more than one child and one of them took the offer to wait for your promise, great. That will make the ones who went for the immediate gratification feel worse. If the kids continue to protest, smile and put them in their place.

Hey, I was very clear with the offer. Something small now, or something much bigger later. Can

arrange for dinner to be late. Really late. That shouldn't be too hard. You can offer the candy and soda to hold them over until dinner is ready. The best time may be when the kids are just coming home from school and they're heading for the fridge.

After you have the snacks and you've figured out when to offer them to the kids, there's one more element you'll need to end the devoes in a powerful way.

- Have a $5 bill for each of the kids. You'll need to write on the margin of the bill something like this: "(child's name), you may exchange this $5 bill for a (select an amount) bill any time after the date of (write a date of anywhere from three months to maybe five years from now). Remember: Delayed gratification pays off!" Sign your name on it to make it official.

The amount of money you'll exchange the $5 bill for in whatever time you allotted on the bill is up to you, but make the sum as large as you can afford. You want the kids to see the value of hanging on to the $5 bill for that amount of time. You may even want to get the kids' grandparents involved to help defray the costs.

you imagine how many snacks you could buy for $20? Oh well. That's the choice you made.

There was a very good reason I offered you this deal. But before I tell you that reason, let me share a Bible story with you.

In Genesis 25:19-34 we read about the brothers Esau and Jacob. Even though they were twins, Esau was born first and consequently would be the heir to the birthright.

One day Esau came in from a day outside. He was hungry, sort of like you were when I offered you the snack. Anyway, he saw Jacob, and apparently Jacob had some great-smelling stew cooking over the fire. Esau asked Jacob to give him some of the stew. But Jacob wanted to strike a deal first. He asked Esau to trade him the firstborn birthright in exchange for the stew.

Esau was so hungry that he let his appetite do the thinking instead of his brain. Esau sold his birthright, worth who knows how much, for a plate of stew. He made a huge mistake. Later he would weep with regret. He became bitter and even thought of murdering Jacob.

So, what is the lesson of this story?

 Let's see what they say. They may talk about bad choices or bad deals; that's fine. Let's make sure that they really understand it.

Tie It Together

Just because Esau was hungry didn't mean he should have sold his birthright to get something to eat. Many times we do something similar in real life, though. There are times when God wants us to be patient. He wants us to hold off on feeding our "appetites" now in exchange for something much better later. The candy was my way of trying to illustrate that truth to you. What are some things you can think of that God may want you to wait on?

Get some input here. Be ready to add in some things that are appropriate for your kids' age levels. If they are in sixth grade or higher, don't avoid the topic of sex. Work through some examples with them.

OK, let's say you want friends. Sometimes we have to wait on the Lord to provide us with a good friend. How might some kids jump the gun on this?

See what they say. You want to hear something along the lines of the fact that some kids try to fit in and end up compromising in some way; they sell themselves short.

How about money, success, "things"? How have you seen other kids or adults be impatient in those areas?

They've seen kids cheat to get better grades. They've probably heard of corporate executives who lied, cheated and basically stole from stockholders to satisfy their greedy appetites.

How about sex? God designed it to be reserved for marriage. Plenty of kids get impatient, though, and want to satisfy their appetites, so they turn to porn or to having sex before they get married. By refusing to be patient, by refusing to do it God's way, they sell themselves way short. The day may come when they find themselves weeping with regret, just like Esau did.

I know, I know—sex can be uncomfortable to talk about with the kids. Get over it. This is far too important to avoid. We have to protect our kids the best we can.

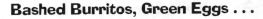

There's something called "delayed gratification." Who can tell me what it means?

If they have an answer here, great. If not, help them out.

Delayed gratification means that you delay gratifying, or you hold off satisfying some desire you have for a greater reward later. Like the candy and soda. If you had held off on satisfying that desire, you'd be holding a $20 certificate right now.

The fact is, our society will urge you to satisfy your every want and desire now. Like Esau exchanging a fortune for a warm plate of stew, there are horrible consequences if you do.

The Bible is full of stories of people who satisfied their urges instead of holding out for the greater reward. David and Bathsheeba are one example. David had a night of pleasure followed by a lifetime of regret and consequences.

The Bible also tells us of some people who did it right. Take Joseph, for example. His master's wife threw herself at him, but he did the right thing and ran away from her. If he hadn't, the very course of his life would have changed. I doubt he would have ended up ruling Egypt if he hadn't resisted the urge to give in to temptation.

Let's take this one step deeper. Esau didn't value his birthright as much as he did a hot plate of stew. That was a slap in the face to his father, don't you think?

Now, we as Christians are the firstborn, the heirs of Christ. Oftentimes we want to live for the "here and now." We aren't curbing our appetites. We aren't living as we should. That's a slap in the face to God. By satisfying our appetites now instead of waiting for God's timing, it shows God that we don't value Him or His plan for us enough to delay our gratification. This is serious stuff!

At this point you've gone longer than you would normally go. You need to wrap this up before they start drifting away. This is the time to do the $5 challenge.

I have a $5 bill for each of you. Now, if you'll look on the border, I've written something on it. It says your name and the following statement: "You may exchange this $5 bill any time after (date and year) for a (larger amount) bill. Remember: Delayed gratification pays off!" The statement is signed by me.

Now, you can keep this safe and bring it back to me any time after the date written on the bill, and I'll exchange it for (whatever the amount was that you decided on), just like I wrote. Or you can buy $5 of junk with this and lose out later. The choice is yours.

You may get a mixed reaction here. They'll be excited about the potential money, but frustrated that they have to wait so long. Hey, it's a good lesson in life.

God's Word is your guide as to how to live. Often there are things we are told to wait on, like sex before marriage. Delayed gratification, not giving in to our appetites before we should, can pay off in more ways than you can imagine. Trust God and do it His way, OK?

Working It into the Week

Here are some verses and passages you may want to jot down for the kids to look at during the week. You may want to point out

that Psalm 51 was David's expression of repentance and remorse after he sinned with Bathsheba.

Day 1: 2 Corinthians 4:18

Day 2: Psalm 51

Day 3: Genesis 39

Day 4: Hebrews 11:24-26

Day 5: Galatians 4:3-7

Day 6: Hebrews 12:1-3

Tools of the Trade

What's the Point?

We'll use some unbelievable newspaper stories to prime a discussion on honesty.

Things You'll Need

- You'll need to pick up several issues of those tabloid newspapers that you see in the racks at the grocery store checkout line. You know what I mean—the ones with the utterly ridiculous headlines on the front cover that you just can't help but read.

Now, I looked through several to get enough material for one devotional, and you might have to do the same. You'll be looking for those bizarre stories that can't possibly be true. You want something that any person with his brain even half engaged will recognize as being a bogus story.

As you find a story that meets the criteria, clip it out and save it for family devoes. You'll want at least two stories for every one of the kids who will be in the devoes.

I'd avoid stories that revolve around celebrities. They get so gossipy, and that isn't where we're going with this. I wouldn't let the kids just browse through the newspaper either. There can be a lot of raunchy stuff in there.

Also, pick up a little pocket flashlight for each of the kids. You can

Here We Go

Have your stories all clipped out before devotions. I didn't have any trouble finding some prime examples of bogus reporting. There was an article about a Chinese plot to reverse the Earth's orbit by having all the Chinese people jump at the same time. There was an article claiming that two of Jesus' disciples were women. It referred to "experts" who suspect that Judas was really named Judith. There was a report, along with a photo, of a dolphin that had grown human hands and feet. There was even a claim of a weeping Elvis statue, and they had the pictures to back it up.

You want to pick stories that leave little doubt about how truthful the article is or, more accurately, isn't. Get the kids together and say something like this:

I have some newspaper articles here that I'd like you to look over. In fact, I'd like each of you to pick out a couple of articles and read them over, and then I'll ask you to give a little report on one of the articles to the rest of us. All you need to do is give us an overview of the story and your opinion of whether the reporter is being completely honest or not, OK?

Answer any questions they may have and let them pick out and read the articles. You can expect a lot of laughs as they leaf through the articles. If they're talking about them out loud or looking over each other's shoulders, fine. The more they get into it, the better.

When the time is right, ask each one to share one of the articles he picked. If they forget to tell you if they think the reporter was being totally truthful, ask them. You might even ask them to back up their opinions with quotes from the articles. Remember, teenagers don't always like giving the obvious answer. Don't be surprised if one of your kids tells you with a straight face that he believes the article he read. Don't try to argue with him. Roll with it.

They'll be enjoying this part of devoes, so you can let them run with it a bit. Be careful not to go too long, though. Even a fun activity can get old. When you've given each of them time to share their conclusions on the articles they picked, move on.

OK, so you can't believe everything you read, I guess. This stuff is a combination of half-truths and outright lies. Why do you suppose people write stuff like this?

See what they say. There are plenty of reasons. Recap a few of them.

I imagine some people write ridiculous stuff like this just for fun. The newspaper prints stories like this because its owners aren't interested in the truth; they just want to make more money by selling more papers.

A lot of people are like that. They tell others what they think they want to hear, and it isn't always the truth. There may be a little truth to it, but it isn't the whole truth. You've probably seen a lot of that at school. Can any of you think of an example?

See what they say here. Don't get nervous if they draw a blank or just don't want to share. Talking about being truthful can get a little uncomfortable. Everyone has secrets that they'd rather keep hidden.

Well, I don't think I have to tell you what God thinks about lies. The real question is, why is it that people lie so much? Why do they tell only part of the truth?

Let's see if they open up here. This is a pretty non-threatening question. You're looking for responses like: Sometimes people lie

find them in any hardware store. Be sure to get the type that allows you to change the batteries. The sealed type won't work as well for our purposes. Pick up enough batteries to power up each of the flashlights, but don't put them in yet.

After you bring the little flashlights home, you'll want to write something on the side of them. Here's what I wrote on ours: "Let truth be a light to guide your way." You can use a fine-point permanent marker, or just write it on a piece of paper and tape it to the sides of the flashlights.

to keep themselves out of trouble. Sometimes they lie to make themselves look better than they are, to impress someone else. They may call it "exaggeration," but it is a form of dishonesty. People often lie to get what they want from another person.

Yep, there are plenty of "good" reasons why people lie. There are at least two really good reasons not to lie, though: God hates lies and punishes liars.

Let me read you some verses from the Bible:

> There are six things the LORD hates,
>   seven that are detestable to him:
>   haughty eyes,
>   a lying tongue,
>   hands that shed innocent blood.
>   (Proverbs 6:16-17)

> A false witness will not go unpunished,
>   and he who pours out lies will not go free.
>   (Proverbs 19:5)

> Whoever of you loves life
>   and desires to see many good days,
> keep your tongue from evil
>   and your lips from speaking lies.
> Turn from evil and do good;
>   seek peace and pursue it. (Psalm 34:12-14)

> Do not lie to each other, since you have taken off your old self with its practices and have put on the new self, which is being renewed in knowledge in the image of its Creator. (Colossians 3:9-10)

Tie It Together

The Bible doesn't have a "little white lies are OK" policy. God doesn't overlook it when we tell half-truths. The verses we read were pretty plain regarding God's stance on lies, weren't they?

Lies and deception are trademarks of the devil. They're his "tools of the trade." When we resort to lies, deceptions and half-truths, we're following the devil in his "trade"; we're following the ways of death. It's ironic that we often lie to avoid trouble or to get ahead when the reality is that lies and deception do just the opposite. Isn't that what the Bible is telling us in those verses? So what do we do about it?

They might not expect a question like this now, and they may not be able to answer it, so you're going to help them along a bit.

This is a tough one. Ask God for help and make a commitment to be truthful. Review those verses on honesty and come to grips with the fact that the way to avoid trouble and get ahead is to be completely honest.

When somebody asks you how he looks, be sure to tactfully and lovingly tell the truth. Love is what it all comes down to. Dishonesty, lies, deception and white lies will damage, even destroy relationships. They have no place in genuine love.

Sometimes it isn't the things we say that are dishonest; it's the things we don't say. Sometimes we leave key details out when telling others about something. That's still lying. Sometimes we keep our mouths shut when we should speak up. That can be dishonest too. If we love others, if we want to do it God's way instead of the devil's, we must be 100 percent honest.

This won't come easily. It takes continual practice. Often we're dishonest without even think-

ing about it. It comes naturally to us. Lies, deception and dishonesty are available for the "quick fix." They often seem to be the best option to cover something up so we avoid trouble or get something we want.

Often kids will opt to cheat on a test so they can get a good grade. Like we discussed earlier, we may even lie to protect someone's feelings, like telling him he looks good in an outfit when you don't really think he does. The chances for dishonesty are always around, and often we compromise a bit. It will take some real work to change that scenario in our lives.

OK, that's as close to a sermon as we dare get. We don't have to explain more about what dishonesty is all about; they get it. The thing is, we want them to want to be honest. We want them to seek after it, and I doubt more talking will do it.

We need to wrap this up. You may want to share a story about a time when you were dishonest. Ouch, it hurts to be vulnerable, doesn't it? Maybe it was something you said or did, or something you didn't say or do but should have. Maybe you can relate a story of a time when you were honest, even though you were tempted not to be. Let me tell you, when you tell a story about yourself—especially one where you did something you shouldn't have—it's powerful.

After you share your story, you might want to offer the kids an opportunity to share a story about a friend, an acquaintance or maybe even something they saw in a movie that was a good example of honesty or dishonesty.

Now is the time to pull out the little flashlights. You could tell them something like this:

We talked about some of the devil's "tools of the trade"—lies, deception and dishonesty. God has "tools of the trade" too. Being truthful is one of them. Here's a little flashlight for each of you. I've written this on the side of each one: "Let truth be a light to guide your way." I know each of you wants to be honest in God's sight. I'm hoping this little light will be a reminder.

Give each of them a flashlight. I'm guessing they'll try to turn them on as soon as you give them to them. When they discover that the flashlights don't work, you can sum the devoes up with something like this:

A flashlight without batteries is just a lie. It can't light the way for anybody. Here are batteries for each of your flashlights. I pray that each of you will choose to use God's "tools of the trade," like honesty, when you're tempted to do otherwise. I pray you won't simply *look* like Christians, like the flashlight without batteries, but that you'll live like Christians too.

Nice job. You may even want to pick up another one of those flashlights as a little reminder for yourself. Remember, as parents and grandparents we need to work hard to be good examples to our children.

Working It into the Week

Jot these verses on honesty down on a separate piece of paper for each of the kids to review throughout the week. Be sure you're reading them too—there's some great stuff there!

Day 1: Proverbs 6:16-19

Day 2: Psalm 5:4-6; Proverbs 19:5

Day 3: Psalm 34:11-14

Day 4: John 8:42-47

Day 5: Colossians 3:9-10

Day 6: Leviticus 19:11; Proverbs 30:7-8

New Lesson from an Old Game

What's the Point?

We'll use the game of musical chairs to illustrate the fact that we tend to think of ourselves first. Then we'll show them what the Bible says about being selfish.

Things You'll Need

- All you'll need is some chairs and your TV remote. You'll want sturdy folding chairs or maybe kitchen chairs for this. Avoid chairs with arms if possible.

Remember the games you'd play when you went to a friend's birthday party as a kid? For me it was always the same: hot potato, drop the clothespin in the milk bottle, pin the tail on the donkey and musical chairs.

We're going to use the game of musical chairs and find a practical application for the kids. I know, your kids are a little too old for this game, right? Don't worry, we'll acknowledge it during the devoes. I think they'll still get into the game.

To put a little insurance on it, plan on offering a prize to the winner. Keep it simple, like the winner doesn't have to do some chore he normally would have to do or he gets to go out to a fast-food restaurant for a snack. Whatever. The point is, offer a prize to the winner of the game that will help motivate the kid to play.

Now, we used to play musical chairs with the help of a kiddie LP

Here We Go

The more kids you have for this one, the better. If you only have one child at home, have him invite a friend or two. We've done that in our family devotions. It makes things more fun, and it allows someone else to hear the devoes. If you have other kids over, offer a prize that anyone will appreciate.

The TV remote will work perfectly for musical chairs. The idea is that you can mute the sound or turn off the TV at the touch of a button. Plan to set things up for the game in the room where your TV is. After you call the kids together, you might say something like this:

All right, guys, each of you will need a chair for family devoes. Get a chair from the kitchen and bring it back here.

Line the chairs up in a row side-by-side. Alternate the direction of every other chair. So if the row of chairs is running north and south, you want the first chair facing east, the second facing west and so on for the rest of the row.

Now here's what we're going to do. We're going to play a little game I used to play at probably every birthday party I went to when I was a kid. Now, I know it's a kid's game, but it will work perfectly for our devotional time tonight. Even though this could get a little dangerous with kids your size, we're going to play musical chairs.

If you get protests here, roll with it. They may complain about it. They don't want to be treated like kids. You're not doing that. You're playing a kid's game. That's an important difference.

Anyway, now is when you tell them about the prize for the winner. Is it a free pass to get out of one of their dreaded chores? Are you going to make one of their beds for a week? Is one of them going out for ice cream or a smoothie or something else he'd really like? Whatever it is, make it good. That should heat the competition up a little. If you need to explain how to play musical chairs, handle that now.

I have the TV remote here. You guys are going to march around the chairs as long as I leave the TV turned on. When I turn it off, you need to scramble for a chair. We'll take one practice run; then we'll eliminate one chair.

Go ahead and take them through a trial run. The kids won't take it all that seriously yet. That's fine. Now eliminate one chair.

This time when the TV goes off, one of you is going to be without a chair. The person who isn't sitting in a chair will be out of the game.

Let them march around the chairs a few times and then turn off the TV with the remote. Hopefully you'll see a little pushing and shoving to get to an empty chair. Perfect. That will help you make the point of this lesson. The one left standing, or closer yet, the one sitting on someone else's lap, is out.

OK, one down. Let's pull away another chair and do it again.

After the chair is gone, turn the TV on and let them march. Turn off the TV without warning when you're ready. Or, better yet, have the person who was just eliminated take over the remote. He'll probably love to get a little revenge.

As the kids are eliminated one-by-one, they'll probably forget all about this being a kid's game. I imagine they'll really be scrambling for the empty chairs. Of course, if the kids are totally courteous and offer their chairs to someone else, you don't even have to finish these devoes.

on a record player. We're a little more sophisticated these days. Now you'll use the TV and the remote.

If you're one of those rare families that do not own a TV, go ahead and use the stereo or, if all else fails, sing.

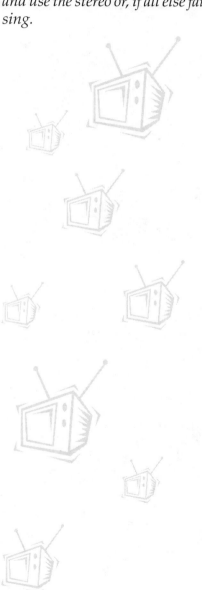

Repeat this procedure until only one person is left. Declare that person as the winner of the prize. If you get some protests from the other kids about how unfair the winner was in the way he played, smile. This is going to work out perfectly. Now it's time to move right into the devoes. You might start out with something like this:

When you're playing this game, you really have to look out for yourself. In fact, most people might have to push and shove a little if they want to get a chair at all. When that TV turns off, somebody is going to be out of the game, and you don't want it to be you.

Let me read you some Bible verses:

> Do nothing out of selfish ambition or vain conceit, but in humility consider others better than yourselves. Each of you should look not only to your own interests, but also to the interests of others. (Philippians 2:3-4)

> Love is patient, love is kind. It does not envy, it does not boast, it is not proud. It is not rude, it is not self-seeking. (1 Corinthians 13:4-5)

Tie It Together

Life can be a lot like musical chairs. We can get so focused on looking out for ourselves that we forget all about our obligations to others. Worse than that, we can even be rude to others or make things hard for others when we're so focused on putting ourselves first. Can anyone give me an example of this kind of behavior?

OK, this is a key moment. They need to see how they do this in the little ways too. If the kids are stuck, you can try to prompt their thinking. The important thing is that they see the light. Unless they can recognize when they're acting out of total selfishness, they will find it difficult to change.

Be ready with a list of examples for them. You may find that the older kids in the family have a tendency to push the younger ones around a little when it comes to getting their own way. There are tons of examples of putting oneself first: Insisting on watching a TV program one wants, interrupting a conversation, pushing one's rights, having a "Hey, I was here first" attitude.

When you get right down to it, many arguments have the "me first" mentality at their roots. Anyway, after the kids mention all they can think of, you can bring up some of the ones mentioned in the previous paragraph or other examples that come to your mind.

Be careful not to use examples that will single out one of the kids or embarrass them too much. You can play it safe by giving examples from another family that you've observed, or by mentioning things that you've done that were selfish.

When you've covered enough examples, move on. You don't want them to start tuning you out just as you get to the application of the devotional.

The truth is, we tend to look out for our own interests a lot more than we should. That isn't the way God says we should do it. He wants us to put others first. That includes brothers and sisters too. Instead of being so concerned about getting what I want, I need to think about others. That may mean I have to give up something for the sake of someone else.

Jesus is our example in this. He gave up heaven to live on Earth as a man. Why? Not because Earth was a better place to live. No, it was because He loved us enough to give up His

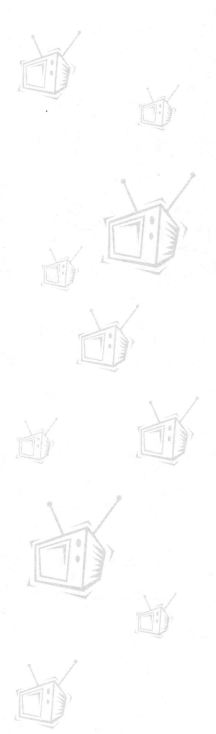

comfort in order to save us. He sacrificed for our good. How can we do that in our own lives?

OK, it's time to see if they're catching the concept. You'll know by their answers. If they have it, you'll want to wrap things up here. If not, you should review a few more examples before you hang it up. Don't expect any of them to totally get this and flawlessly put it into practice. I wish it were that easy, but this is something we all struggle with. In fact, that's probably a good thing to tell the kids.

You know, this is a very difficult thing to do. I still struggle with putting myself first more often than I'd like to admit. This is something that you'll have to fight all your life, so you might as well start now. Jesus lived a totally unselfish life. That's how He wants us to live. And the thing is, it's a better way to live.

OK, I think you're done. Watch for things this week that you can use to reinforce the truth of today's lesson. Maybe you see someone putting himself first at work or in a fast-food line some-place. Tell the kids what you saw when you get home. Ask them what they think. Ask them how they think the person should have acted. You get the idea. Reinforcement is the key.

Don't forget to point out good examples as well as bad. When you see someone doing it right, tell the kids what you observed. There are plenty of Bible examples too. This is powerful stuff.

You might want to ask the kids to observe things this week too. Then they can share their observations with you and the rest of the family. That would really reinforce what they've learned. Try not to turn it into a tattling scenario, though. It will be less poten-tially volatile if they give examples of things they've observed in friends or kids from school.

Working It into the Week

Here are some verses to help reinforce the topic of selfishness during the week. You might want to jot the references down on a separate sheet of paper for each of the kids. Have them add it to their personal devotional times.

Day 1: Proverbs 18:1; Philippians 2:3-4

Day 2: 1 Corinthians 10:24

Day 3: 1 Corinthians 13:4-5

Day 4: 1 Corinthians 10:33

Day 5: Matthew 19:21

Day 6: Psalm 119:36; 2 Corinthians 8:9

I Wouldn't Say That

What's the Point?

Because love is not rude, there are some things we just shouldn't say or do to others. We'll use a game show approach to get the kids thinking along those lines.

Things You'll Need

You won't need anything in particular for this one, but you will want to think some things through in advance of your devotional time.

You'll be playing a "game show" as an activity. We've written down some sample questions below, but you may want to add more questions and categories, especially if you have more kids participating in the devotional.

You'll also need to be thinking of a prize. The person who answers the most questions right will be the winner. Since the answers to the questions are very obvious, you may have a tie for first place. That's OK. Just keep that in mind when you're deciding what you want to do for a prize. The prizes don't have to be elaborate, but they need to be appealing. You could offer the winner(s) pizza for the following evening or maybe a free pass to get out of doing one of their least favorite chores around the house.

If there won't be more than one child playing the game, tell your child he needs to get at least (pick a number that you think will work, like seven out of ten) questions correct in order to get the prize.

Here We Go

You're going to get the kids together to play a little game called "I Wouldn't Say That." Here's how to play: You'll give each of the kids a turn to answer one of the questions you'll read out loud. Explain that you'll read the different categories, like "At School" or "At the Airport." Once they select a category, read a statement to them and ask them to tell you if the statement is something they would or would not say. The answers will be extremely obvious—they should all be "I wouldn't say that."

Here's a list of categories and sample statements. If you feel a statement isn't appropriate for your kids, don't use it. You may even want to add to the list.

At the Airport

1. Wow, this backpack is heavy. I never knew a bomb could weigh so much!

2. I have no idea where this suitcase came from. Some guy outside gave me $20 to check it on the plane with my luggage.

At the Bank

1. Give me all the cash in your drawer.

2. This is a holdup.

At School

1. Sometimes I get so angry, I could shoot someone!

2. Those kids have made me feel stupid too many times. Very soon they'll be sorry, yeah, they'll all be sorry!

3. I always carry my dad's pistol in my backpack.

At a Restaurant (said loudly just for a joke)

1. I think I just saw a mouse run out of the kitchen!

2. There's a worm in my salad!

3. There's a wad of hair in my soup!

At the Dinner Table

1. Whoever cooked this meal must be a total idiot. This is the worst meal I've ever had!

2. I was talking to a friend at school. We're thinking of dropping out and joining a traveling carnival when we're sixteen.

3. We just completed a section in health class about the dangers of drugs. I don't know if I buy all the paranoid warnings on it. I mean, how can you really say drugs are bad unless you've tried them?

To Your Boss

1. Wow, I love this job. I just got back from a nap in the stockroom. I get paid to sleep!

2. My friends love the fact that I work at a fast-food restaurant. They're always coming in for free food!

To Your Date's Dad (if you're a boy)

1. You have a curfew for your daughter? Gee, I usually stay out as late as I want with the other girls I date.

To Your Date's Mom (if you're a girl)

1. I think it would be so cool to have a baby before I graduate from high school!

If You Were a Doctor Talking to a Patient Just Before Surgery

1. This is a relatively simple surgery, which is good because I haven't tried it in years.

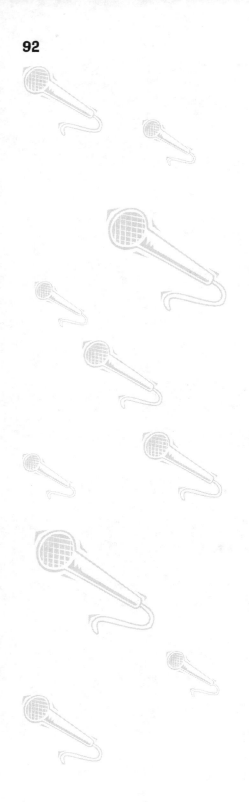

2. We'll be trying a new type of surgery on you today. In fact, I was just reading about it last night, and I said, "Gee, I have to try this technique on someone."

3. Hey, be happy you get to sleep during the surgery today. I was up all night. I could fall asleep standing up!

4. Let's hope this week is a better week for surgery. Last week I messed up almost every operation I did.

If You Were a Nurse in a Maternity Ward

1. Uh-oh. I shouldn't have taken the name bands off. Which one is which?

2. I've seen some homely babies before, but yours takes the cake!

If You Were a Teacher Talking to Parents at a School Open House

1. The truth is, I really hate kids.

Here's how you might start things out once you have the kids together.

Well, for devoes we're going to play a little game. I'm going to ask each of you to select a category, like "At School" or "At the Airport." Once you select the category, I'm going to read you a statement. After I read the statement, all you have to do is to say either, "I would say that" or "I wouldn't say that." Got it?

Make sure they're tracking here. If you need to read one statement as a sample, go ahead.

The one who has answered the most questions correctly will be our winner. Now, to make this a little more interesting, there will be a prize for the winner. Let me tell you about your prize.

This is when you tell them about getting the pizza or giving the winner a free pass not to do some specific chore or whatever. You want the prize to be a good enough incentive for the kids to respond to the statements correctly.

Once you've explained how to play, go ahead and start. Have the first child pick a category; then read the statement and get his response. Keep track of how they do. They should get everything right. Then again, teenagers may try to frustrate you by giving the wrong answer. That's fine. Just roll with it. Give each of the kids a turn.

Go a second and third round if you have enough statements left. Repeat this procedure until there are no statements left. Your kids will probably enjoy this—they may even come up with some scenarios of their own of things they shouldn't say in specific places. That would be great if they did. Let's keep moving.

Hopefully, they answered everything correctly and the winner(s) will officially be told that he's earned his prize(s). Let's transition into the meat of the devoes by saying:

OK, you've proven to me that you have plenty of common sense when it comes to things you shouldn't say if you want to stay out of trouble.

There are other things we say, though, that can cause a whole different kind of trouble. I'm referring to being rude to people who we're supposed to love. Brothers, sisters, parents and friends are often wounded by rude things we say or do. Can anyone give me an example?

Hopefully you'll get some input, but don't let it get into a finger-pointing brawl. You need to get some examples here. If they don't come up with any, have a list of your own handy. Read some of them and ask the kids how it makes them feel when someone makes a rude comment to them like that.

Here are a couple of ideas of rude things kids say or do. Add some of your own examples to the list so you have something to prompt the kids' minds if they can't think of anything.

- Telling someone he's stupid (not in a joking way).

- Interrupting a younger sibling and acting like he isn't important to you in any way.

- Talking fresh to a parent or someone in authority.

- Making fun of people who have a problem (weight, clumsiness, looks, whatever).

- Being opinionated and critical of someone else.

- Thinking about yourself first.

Let me share some Bible verses with you:

Love is patient, love is kind. It does not envy, it does not boast, it is not proud. It is not rude. (1 Corinthians 13:4-5)

Reckless words pierce like a sword, but the tongue of the wise brings healing.
(Proverbs 12:18)

A wise man's heart guides his mouth.
(Proverbs 16:23)

He who guards his mouth and his tongue keeps himself from calamity.
(Proverbs 21:23)

For out of the overflow of the heart the mouth speaks. (Matthew 12:34)

If anyone considers himself religious and yet does not keep a tight rein on his tongue, he deceives himself and his religion is worthless. (James 1:26)

Tie It Together

When we hear these verses, we can see that love should not be rude in actions or words. We also discover that the words we say mirror our hearts. If we're being rude, we have a heart problem.

Being rude is worse than simply displaying bad manners. It's wrong, and that means it is sin.

That verse in Proverbs 21 tells us that the person who guards his tongue saves himself from calamity or trouble. That's especially true when it comes to relationships with others and with God. God tells us that we aren't to be rude in what we say or what we do, and that there are consequences if we ignore that. Can you think of any examples of being rude to someone?

See what they say here. If they're quiet, that's OK too. How about you? Do you sometimes slip and say or do something rude to people you're supposed to love? If you do, you can guarantee that the kids see it. You know how being rude generally adds "calamity" to your life. It can heat up an argument, can't it?

You may need to commit to working on this yourself. Now let's wrap it up. The kids have gotten the message, and spending more time on it will only diminish its effect.

Being rude in the way we act or in the way we speak is more than poor manners. It's wrong and it causes trouble for us and pain for others. God doesn't want rudeness to be part of our lives. Let's be more considerate of each other. Before you say or do something, try to think about how it will affect the people you're supposed to be loving. Will you work on it?

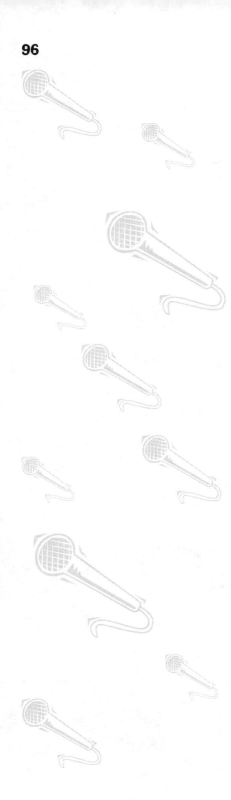

A nod is plenty when it comes to a response from the kids. Ask God to help you be aware of times when you may be rude to the kids. Sometimes we can get sloppy as parents and we can come across as seeming pretty rude. The kids will be watching. When you realize something you did or said was rude, apologize for it. That will go a long way toward reinforcing this lesson.

Working It into the Week

Here are some additional verses on the topic you may want to jot down on a separate piece of paper for each of the kids. You don't have to write out the whole verse; just the reference is fine. There are some good reminders here, so be sure you're looking up the verses too!

Day 1: Matthew 12:33-37; 15:17-20

Day 2: Psalm 34:11-16

Day 3: Psalm 37:30-31

Day 4: Psalm 141:3-4

Day 5: Proverbs 10:11; 19:28-29

Day 6: Proverbs 12:18; 16:23-24; 21:23; James 1:26

OUTDOOR DEVOTIONALS

Follow That Car

What's the Point?

Love has a duty to protect others, and one way to protect a person you love is to help him avoid stumbling blocks in his life. This car ride will get the point across as smoothly as the road you'll be driving on.

Things You'll Need

• This one will be easy as far as preparation is concerned. All you'll need is the car.

Here We Go

Here's the idea: You'll get the kids together and simply say that you'll be taking a little ride in the car for family devotions. The first question they'll have is, "Where are we going?" You can simply smile and shrug. Tell them you have no idea.

When everybody is buckled in, start up the car and explain what you're going to do, but don't tell them why. You might say something like this:

We're going to pull out on the road, and I'd like one of you to pick a car for me to follow.

Pause here to savor the mild confusion on their part. They'll have questions, so you'll need to explain just a little bit more.

I want you to pick a car and point it out to me. Then I'm going to follow it wherever it goes. If we get bored with that car, we can switch to another car at any time. It's up to you. If we do this right, we'll be following a perfect stranger, and he'll have no idea he's being tailed.

Have some fun with this. If it's still light out, you may want to slip on a pair of sunglasses and look around in a furtive manner. You'll also want to explain that if a car is going too fast or if it pulls into a driveway, they'll have to pick a new car for you to tail.

Pick one of the kids to choose a car. They'll have to pick quickly if you're pulling into traffic. I'd avoid the big highways if you can. If you pick a car there, it may get boring if the car is driving straight for miles and miles. Local roads will probably be more interesting. As you're following the car, you might want to ask why they chose that car. Was it the color, the model, the person driving it? If they don't have an answer, don't press it.

Keep a safe distance from the target car and enjoy. Have the kids help you watch where the car is going if you get separated at all. If the car pulls into a grocery store parking lot, pull in right behind it. Now it's up to the kids. Ask them if they want to pick a new car or wait for your driver to come back. Stay flexible with this and the kids will love it. Normally we're in such a hurry when we're in the car. This will be very different for them.

If the car you're following is getting a little dull, you may want to switch cars at some point. You don't want the kids to get bored, so you'll have to know when to pull the plug.

Here's a great way to end it. Tell them you're going to switch cars and this time you'll do the picking. Drive along an area that has fast-food restaurants and watch for a car that is pulling into the drive-thru lane. As you see the car pulling in, point it out and say, "That's my car!"

Pull in right behind the car. When it's time to order, tell the order-taker that you'd like exactly what the car ahead of you ordered. The kids won't believe it. When they hand you the food and drinks, pull into a parking space and divide out the food. That ought to be interesting. You may have too much food or not enough. The kids will think you've really lost it. While they're eating, you can start to talk.

Well, that was fun. I don't think any one of the drivers we followed had a clue that we were tailing them. Which car did you like following the best?

This could be interesting. It would be great if they mentioned a particular kind of car they liked. Maybe it will be where a car went that will turn out to be the most interesting. Certainly the car in the fast-food drive-thru ought to rank up there. Anyway, you may be able to use this information later.

You're still wondering why we did this, right? Let me explain. You chose a car based on its style or because of some other feature. We followed it

Don't Scare Anyone

As you're doing this devoes be sure that you don't freak out the person you're following. If they start making wild turns down one-way streets, it's probably time to either choose another car to follow or call it quits.

wherever it went. The driver didn't even know someone was watching his every move, right?

Well, that's a lot like life. Each of us follow people in our lives. Some people we follow for a long time, others for a shorter time. Sometimes we pick people because of the way they look. They're handsome or cute or popular or athletic. We go where they go, we do what they do and we dress like they dress, at least to some degree. We often start talking like they talk.

Sometimes there's nothing wrong with imitating someone in that way. It's harmless. Other times it could be disastrous. It all depends on who you follow and what that person does, right?

Give them a moment to process this. They probably have someone in mind right now. Don't expect much of an answer here. Move on.

Let me read some verses from the Bible:

> Do not be misled: "Bad company corrupts good character." (1 Corinthians 15:33)

> My son, if sinners entice you,
>   do not give in to them. (Proverbs 1:10)

Tie It Together

I certainly don't have to go into a lot of explanation on being careful about who you choose to follow or imitate. We've talked about the dangers of that before. This is just a reminder. Even Solomon, the wisest man in the world, lost sight of that. He disobeyed God by marrying all those women, yet somehow he must have felt he was an exception to the rule and that he wouldn't be affected by their godless influence. Obviously he was wrong, and First Kings 11 tells us how the women turned Solomon's heart away from God.

Solomon's son didn't learn from his father's mistake. When faced with a big decision in First Kings 12, he didn't consult God. He talked to his father's old advisors and he talked with his friends. He preferred the counsel of the guys his age. Unfortunately, he got some bad advice, and most of the country rebelled against him.

Like I said, we know this stuff. But let's take it a step further. When we read about genuine love in First Corinthians 13:7, it tells us that love "protects." What do you think that means? How do we "protect" those we love?

You want a little feedback here. Don't worry if they go off on a tangent. They may give you what you're looking for, but it's more likely that they won't. A lot of their answers are probably good ones, but steer them to where you want to go.

One aspect of "protecting" those you love is watching out for them. You have a responsibility to help each other stay on the right paths. In a nice way—and that's extremely important—you might have to help someone you love see that the route he's heading down, or the person he's following, is not good for him. Does that make sense?

Get their response to this. You may even want to share a story about how someone tried to protect you that way once, or maybe how you tried to protect someone else. So far the devotional hasn't been all that convicting. But that's about to end.

Let's take this one final step deeper. What if the person leading someone you love astray is

you? Think about it and ask yourself, "How am I living?" If someone follows you in the things you say and do, if he were to adopt your attitudes, if he were to allow your compromises, would he be going down the "right" road?

Here's a scary passage in the Bible. Jesus is speaking.

> "Things that cause people to sin are bound to come, but woe to that person through whom they come. It would be better for him to be thrown into the sea with a millstone tied around his neck than for him to cause one of these little ones to sin. So watch yourselves." (Luke 17:1-3)

It's bad enough when *we* screw up and go the wrong way. It's much worse when others follow us. The thing is, we don't always know when someone is following us, do we? I mean, the drivers in those cars we followed didn't seem to be aware of us, did they? The same thing happens with us. People are watching—friends, acquaintances and especially younger kids, like a brother or sister. The key is, we usually aren't aware that they're following us.

In First Timothy 4:12, we're told to "set an example for the believers in speech, in life, in love, in faith and in purity." We need to help protect others. That's a big responsibility, but I know we can do it. One way we can do it is to help keep others on the right road by staying there ourselves. I'm praying that you'll do just that.

OK, it would be nice to get some discussion here, but I think they've got it. We don't need to overwork it.

Working It into the Week

I'd have some Scripture references written out on a separate piece of paper for each of the kids to review during the week. Here are some suggestions:

Day 1: 1 Kings 11:1-6

Day 2: 1 Corinthians 15:33

Day 3: Proverbs 1:10

Day 4: Luke 17:1-3

Day 5: 1 Corinthians 13:6-7

Day 6: 1 Timothy 4:12

Bashed Burritos

What's the Point?

The kids will get a very graphic demonstration of the mess anger makes. Its effect isn't limited to the person who "flies off the handle," but it nails everyone within range.

Things You'll Need

- You'll need a baseball bat (wooden or aluminum preferably—a plastic whiffle ball bat just won't have the "oomph" you want for this).

- At least two or three burritos per child in the devotional and some wide-open spaces.

This will get messy, so you may not want to wear your favorite clothes for this one, and you should probably encourage the kids to dress in "grungy" clothes as well.

I'd pick up the burritos at a fast-food restaurant where you can get them cheap. Don't skimp on the quantity here. The kids will love this, and I guarantee they'll want to smash more than one burrito each.

Here We Go

Get the kids together, pile them into the car and go out to pick up the burritos. When you're ordering at the drive-thru window, some of the kids may protest a little. They might not like burritos, or they might want you to order something else for them. If you order anything else, that's up to you, but I'd just order a bunch of burritos and make them wonder what you're up to.

You'll have to do a little explaining to the kids when you get to the spot you've selected for batting practice. You might say something like this:

I know you're wondering what we're going to do with all these burritos, so let me explain. We're going to play a little "burrito baseball." Here's how it works. I'm going to be the pitcher, and each of you is going to have a turn at bat. Instead of pitching a ball to you, I'm going to pitch a burrito. The object is to see how far the bashed bits of burrito fly after you bat it. Any questions?

I would expect there's a little excitement going on about now. They may not be sure how far they can bash a burrito, but they're pretty sure the bits will make it to the pitcher. How often do they get a chance like this to nail Mom or Dad?

Once you get to your designated location, let your first batter get into position. You'll probably have to stay closer to the batter than the normal pitcher's mound. First of all, you can't pitch a burrito very far, and second, you want to make sure some of the burrito hits you. That's right. This isn't something you can run and hide from. If you end up wearing a few burrito bits, the kids will love it!

You may want to sling a rubber band around each burrito before you pitch it. You don't want it to fall apart before your batter gets a whack at it. Now, pitch that burrito nice and easy. You want the kids to be able to hit it. Put a nice arc on it. If your kids aren't very consistent with their hitting, let them take a few practice swings with something other than the burrito. When they're warmed up, pitch 'em the burrito. Now, if they miss, scoop the burrito back up and pitch it again. They need to connect.

When they do connect, I'm hoping you look like you just walked out of a Mexican restaurant in the middle of a food fight. Sour cream, refried beans and rice ought to be everywhere. When they nail you, feel free to duck or scream, but don't run. When the kids see the burrito bits in your hair, it will ratchet the excitement up a couple of notches.

Continue this procedure for each of your batters until all the burritos are gone. Take a minute to inspect the mess with the kids. You should be wearing a fair amount of the burritos yourself. Hopefully, the kids caught some of the splatters too. Perfect. Now you're ready to talk about anger. The fact is, when someone gets angry, people are going to get messed up. You might start out by saying something like this:

Well, that was messy. I know you might have enjoyed this, but I don't think I'll be begging to pitch burritos to you again any time soon. I'm probably going to have nightmares about exploding burritos.

There's another kind of explosion that can be just as messy, and it can cause a lot of nightmares too. I'm talking about anger. What do you think is the real root behind anger?

Let's get them thinking here. We're trying to get them to recognize that anger often stems from pride, a "how could they treat me like that?" mentality. See what they come up with. If they don't bring up pride, that's OK. You can just say something like:

When you get down to the bottom of it all, it seems to me that a lot of anger really stems from a pride problem. Maybe we don't feel we've been given the respect or attention we deserve. Pride. Maybe somebody had the nerve to give me a raw deal. Me! Pride again. Pride is sin, and sometimes it's good to remember that pride is at the root of most angry outbursts. Let me read a few Bible verses:

> A fool gives full vent to his anger,
> but a wise man keeps himself
> under control. (Proverbs 29:11)

> A wise man fears the LORD and shuns evil,
> but a fool is hotheaded and reckless.
> A quick-tempered man does foolish things.
> (Proverbs 14:16-17)

> My dear brothers, take note of this: Everyone should be quick to listen, slow to speak and slow to become angry, for man's anger does not bring about the righteous life that God desires. (James 1:19-20)

> Like a city whose walls are broken down
> is a man who lacks self-control.
> (Proverbs 25:28)

> In your anger do not sin: Do not let the sun go down while you are still angry. (Ephesians 4:26)

Tie It Together

Anger has a way of affecting other people. Take our burrito baseball game, for instance— the pitcher got nailed! Anger is like that. One person in the family gets angry and other people in the family get hurt by something that the angry person says or does. Can anyone give me an example of this kind of effect?

Get ready. It could be that the person they'll mention is you. Yes, even parents can make a mess of things. In any case, just listen to what the kids are saying—don't try to defend anyone just yet. We're trying to get their minds engaged here. If this turns into a tattling session, you may have to play referee and get things back on track.

Anger can be more than just an explosion. It can also be a lack of self-control. That verse in Ephesians that I just read acknowledges that we are going to get angry sometimes. The key, however, is not to sin when we do get angry. We have to control our tempers and our mouths, or we'll have a mess on our hands. That verse tells us not to just hold the anger in either, because then we're headed for bitterness or a really bad explosion.

First Corinthians 13:5 tells us that real love isn't easily angered. That's how God loves us, with a perfect love, and that's how we're supposed to love others. How can we do that?

That's the million-dollar question, isn't it? If you're married, you can probably see how many times you don't really love your spouse as you should, at least not when it comes to the "love is not easily angered" part. We have to put up with the little irritations and not let ourselves get angry over it.

Anyway, see what the kids say here. Conquering anger doesn't come naturally with age. We've all seen too many crabby old people to believe that. It needs to be a matter of prayer and deliberate effort to make some progress in this area. We can't do it on our own, which is why we have the Holy Spirit to help us. Take whatever they give you and build on it.

It will take some effort on your part to conquer anger. That means it starts with prayer. It's well worth it, though. Not only will it make things a little less messy at home, but it will help you in the future too, especially in a marriage. Learning to love others enough not to get easily angered is God's plan, and He'll bless your efforts.

Time to end this before the kids get angry with you.

Working It into the Week

Here are some references for verses on this whole anger issue. You can jot them on a separate piece of paper for each of the kids for use as a prep for this devotional or for the week after the devotional as a review.

Day 1: Ephesians 4:26-27

Day 2: 1 Corinthians 13:4-5

Day 3: Proverbs 25:28

Day 4: James 1:19-20

Day 5: Proverbs 29:11, 22

Day 6: Proverbs 14:16-17

A Bunch of "Do's" and "Don'ts"

What's the Point?

We hear all the time that the Christian life is just a bunch of "do's" and "don'ts." We don't want our kids to buy into that lie, and we'll use a lawyer (or at least some law books) to prove our case!

Things You'll Need

- Make a trip in advance to your local library to see if they have a big section of law books. If there is a college in the area, you may find that their library is even better. Talk to the librarian if you need help finding the law section. Ideally they'll have rows of books on all kinds of law—federal, state, corporate, whatever.

- If the library doesn't have a large number of law books, visit a nearby lawyer's office and ask if you can bring your kids in to see how many law books he has. You'll want to explain what you're planning to do, and you can assure him that you won't let the kids touch anything. If he wants you to sign something, go back to the library idea. We've based this devotional on a trip to the library, so you may have to revise it a bit if you end up at a lawyer's office.

- On the day you actually do your family devotions you'll need to have your Bible handy.

Here We Go

Pile the kids into the car and tell them you just want to show them something before you bring them back home for family devotions. Drive to the library.

Take the kids right to the law books. Speak in a quiet tone—there's a sort of sacred air about law books. Explain to the kids what is in front of them (books on federal law, state law, etc.).

Have them count how many volumes are on the shelf. When they're done counting, have everybody troop up to the help desk and ask the librarian if the library has all of the books on United States law or if there are more. You'll want the kids to hear the answer to that question. Then have everybody go back to the law section and pick up a book and flip through it—carefully. Point out the fine print and the fact that there are no pictures.

When you think the kids have a feel for the tonnage of laws, thank your librarian and leave. You may want to go home or just go to a fast-food place, get them each a drink and some fries and talk there. Place your Bible on the table when you sit down. You might start out by saying something like this:

Did you have any idea there could be so many books full of laws?

You may not get more than a head shake for a response. That's OK. Move on.

There are a lot more laws out there than we can imagine, and I wanted you to see it for yourself so you'd know the truth.

Pause for a moment like you think they know exactly what you're talking about. They probably don't, unless they've been looking at this book. See if someone asks the question, "The truth about what?" If they don't, just answer the question anyway.

The truth about God's Word and about Christianity. Does anybody know what I mean?

They may guess, but I doubt they have it yet. You're trying to get them to think instead of them simply waiting for you to spoon-feed them. Hopefully their minds are starting to get into gear. Keep moving.

Well, people who are not Christians have often accused Christians of following a bunch of "do's" and "don'ts." They feel we're all locked up tight in a restrictive religious system of laws and regulations that govern our lives. That is one example of how the devil can twist the truth.

Regular law books are full of restrictions. They are all about rights and legal boundaries and what happens when someone crosses those boundaries. Listen to a couple of verses from our "law book," the Bible:

> Jesus did many other miraculous signs in the presence of his disciples, which are not recorded in this book. But these are written that you may believe that Jesus is the Christ, the Son of God, and that by believing you may have life in his name. (John 20:30-31)

God gave us the Bible because He wanted to save us from a wasted life and an eternity in hell. You call that restrictive? Hardly. It sounds a whole lot more like freedom to me. No wonder the devil wants people to think the Bible is a bunch of "do's" and "don'ts." He doesn't want anybody to be set free.

Tie It Together

Even if the whole Bible were nothing but laws from cover to cover, even if there were no stories

in here or things to encourage us and strengthen us, there still would only be one book here. That's one book compared to dozens and dozens of law books for our state and country.

And the fact is that this whole Book isn't full of laws. There are tons of stories, letters of encouragement, insights and truths to help show us how to live a life full of meaning and satisfaction. It shows us how to be free from the guilt of sin and how to avoid the traps of the devil.

It explains how we can trust God and be free from worry. It teaches us how to avoid things that will hurt us. It reveals that we don't need to be imprisoned by fear because God is always with us and He will never leave us. It teaches us about God's great love for us and how we can know we have eternal life. The Bible strengthens us and protects us.

Sure, there are things we're supposed to do and things we're to avoid, but even in that regard Jesus was able to boil it all down to one brief statement. It all has to do with love. It's about God's great love for us and His desire that we love Him and love other people.

Now, that doesn't mean that living the way the Bible teaches is easy. Loving God and loving others is something that takes work. Being free from fear and worry doesn't happen overnight. It doesn't all just come naturally. God knows that, which is why He gave us the Bible and His Spirit to help teach us how we should live.

The Bible is much more than harsh "do's" and "don'ts." It has a lot more to do with positive things, like being kind, patient and loving. So my prayer for you is that you become a great lover of God and people. I pray that you will love God's Word, the Bible, and make it your guidebook for your lives.

So, the next time you hear someone say that Christianity is just a bunch of "do's" and "don'ts," remember the truth. Why not tell that person that the whole "do's" and "don'ts" thing is a better description of this world.

You can prove it too. You can tell them to stack up all the different books of laws we have in our country alone as compared to Christianity's one "law book," the Bible. It doesn't take a lawyer to figure out which stack is bigger. Christianity only has one Book, and all of the teachings found in it can be boiled down to love. Listen to Matthew 22:36-40:

> "Teacher, which is the greatest command-
> ment in the Law?"
> Jesus replied: " 'Love the Lord your God
> with all your heart and with all your soul
> and with all your mind.' This is the first and
> greatest commandment. And the second is
> like it: 'Love your neighbor as yourself.' All
> the Law and the Prophets hang on these
> two commandments."

I'd like to see a lawyer boil all the law books down to one phrase that would hold up in a court of law.

What do you think about all this?

Whew! We have to stop and get some input from them. We've been talking for a long time, and that's risky when you're trying to hold kids' attention. Let's see what they have to say. You may not get much of a response, but you've certainly given them something to think about. I'll bet it all pops back into their minds the next time they hear someone say that Christianity is a bunch of "do's" and "don'ts."

Working It into the Week

You may want to jot down the following verses on a sheet of paper for each kid and encourage them to read them while they have their personal devotions.

Day 1: Matthew 7:12

Day 2: Matthew 22:36-40

Day 3: John 20:30-31

Day 4: Joshua 1:7-9

Day 5: Romans 13:8-10; 2 Timothy 3:14-17

Day 6: Proverbs 4:13; 8:10-11

Haul of Shame

What's the Point?

We'll demonstrate how "things" can weigh us down and keep us focused on ourselves instead of others. A selfish person can't go as far or as fast as the Lord may have planned for him.

Things You'll Need

- You'll need a wheelbarrow, a wagon or some other kind of cart. If you don't have one, ask a friend or neighbor.

- Next you'll need some weight. I bought a few sixty-pound tubes of sand from the hardware store for under $4 each. Any weight will do. It can be dirt, bricks, rocks or barbell weights, as long as it will fit in the wheelbarrow. How much weight should you have on hand? I'd say at least 100 pounds, and probably closer to 200.

- Make a list of "things" you think your kids would like. After you've made your list, put an approximate weight with each item. Don't worry about the weight being accurate to the pound. Just make a reasonable guess. Here's a sample list:

- 42" TV: 50 lbs.

- VCR player: 8 lbs.

- DVD player: 8 lbs.

- New computer, printer, etc.: 20 lbs.

Here We Go

Get the wheelbarrow and the weights together outside. The plan is this: Before you hand out the "wish list," have each child take a turn running the course with the unladen wheelbarrow. Make sure to track their times so that you can compare them with their runs of the course with the weight-filled wheelbarrow.

Next, have each of the kids look down the list and tell you which things they'd like to have if money wasn't an issue. If there is something they'd like that isn't on the list, add it on with an approximate weight.

Now total each of their "hauls" up and put the appropriate number of weights in the wheelbarrow. Be sure the weight is manageable. If one of your kids puts a car on the list, well, I wouldn't worry about that weight just yet. You don't need to add back problems to your busy week.

When you're ready, get the kids together and say:

OK, I'm going to give each of you a chance to get the things you've always wanted. Of course, this will be kind of an imaginary thing, so don't get your hopes up too high. I want you to look at this list of things I wrote down. If I'm missing something you'd like, let me know and I'll be happy to add it.

You don't have to explain more than that at this point. Get them busy picking out what they want. If you have a separate list for each of them to work on, they'll all be busy at the same time.

As each one finishes, make a quick tally of the weights they'll need. You may not have enough weight for all the things they want. That's OK. We just want to make sure there is enough weight in the wheelbarrow to make it hard for them to handle. Now explain what they have to do.

Here's what we're going to do. You're each going to take two runs of the route I've chosen. The first time you'll take the empty wheelbarrow on the route. I'll be timing you, so go as fast as you can. For the second run, I've assigned a rough estimate of weights to the items on your lists, and I'm going to have each of you take a turn putting the correct amount of weight in the wheelbarrow. Then you'll have to wheel it around the chosen route. This trip is going to be timed too, so go as quickly as you can, but if the wheelbarrow tips over you'll lose everything in it and take a twenty-second penalty.

Go ahead and have them run the route with the empty wheelbarrow. Be sure to keep track of their times. Once they have all run the route with the empty wheelbarrow, have one of the kids load it up with the appropriate amount of weight for all of the stuff that he wanted. If he can't handle the load, go on to the next child. Keep a record of each person's time. You may want to take a picture of them struggling with the wheelbarrow. It will make a nice reminder later.

When everyone has had their turn, find a place for everyone to sit down and talk about it. I'll bet your older kids have already guessed what's coming. That's OK; keep going.

It was pretty tough to run the race with all that weight in the wheelbarrow, wasn't it? As each of you discovered, the more stuff you wanted from the wish list, the more it slowed you down when it came to hauling it around. Let me read some verses from the Bible:

> "Watch out! Be on your guard against all kinds of greed; a man's life does not consist in the abundance of his possessions." (Luke 12:15)

- New bike: 20 lbs.

Keep adding items they'd be interested in until you have a decent-sized list. Keep the master copy for yourself with the weight approximations listed and a copy for each of the kids without any weights listed.

- You'll also want to determine a route that the kids will have to race the wheelbarrow on. You may want them to make a couple of laps around the house or down the block and back. The whole point you want to make here is that the more weight they carry, the harder the hauling gets. All the "things" they want will slow them down.

Therefore, since we are surrounded by such a great cloud of witnesses, let us throw off everything that hinders and the sin that so easily entangles, and let us run with perseverance the race marked out for us. Let us fix our eyes on Jesus, the author and perfecter of our faith. (Hebrews 12:1-2)

Keep your lives free from the love of money and be content with what you have, because God has said,
  "Never will I leave you;
    never will I forsake you."
(Hebrews 13:5)

Tie It Together

It can be really easy to want more and more stuff. The trouble is, it can slow us down when it comes to living the kind of life that God has planned for us.

It seems that the more stuff we have, the less time we have for God and others. If something slows us down in our walks with God, it may come back to haunt us someday.

When we're focused on ourselves and our stuff, we're simply being selfish. When we're selfish, our eyes aren't open to the needs of others, and they certainly aren't on the Lord, either. That definitely isn't the way God wants us to live. When we aren't living the way God wants us to live, we may be headed for danger, don't you think?

We've been talking a lot here. Time for some input from the kids. Let's see what is going on in their minds. Just listen to whatever input they give.

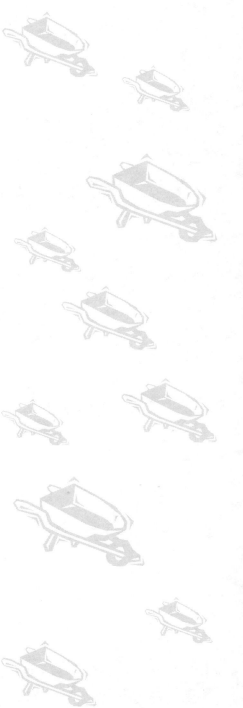

It's natural to want things and to work to get them. But we have to be careful we don't fall into the trap of being selfish and hindering the plans God has for us. When we do have things, we want to use them to serve God in some way. We also want to be generous with others and share.

Selfishness is just a form a greed, and it is wrong. It's something we need to fight. Can any of you give me an example of someone who was selfish or greedy or someone who was unselfish or giving?

We're looking for some input from them, just to reinforce the lesson a bit in their minds. It might take them a minute. Be ready with a list to help jog their thinking. Here are some examples from the Bible that you can give them in case they have trouble coming up with examples:

- Genesis 13-14: Abraham giving Lot first choice when they divided the land.

- 1 Samuel 25: Nabal not willing to share food with David's men.

- 1 Kings 11:1-3: Solomon gathering more riches and wives.

- Hebrews 11:24-25: Moses giving up the riches of Egypt to be with his people.

- Mark 10:37: James and John seeking positions of greater honor for themselves.

You could go on and on here, but don't. You don't want to push it so long that they start to lose interest. Wrap it up.

I want to warn you of the danger of selfishness and encourage you to fight it. Selfishness works against you in so many ways. It will destroy relationships, and it has no place in genuine love.

A selfish person is looking to make a "haul." He's out to get the best deal and the most stuff that he can for himself. He puts himself first. If he continues that way, he'll find that his haul is very heavy indeed. He'll make a haul all right. It will be a haul of shame, though, and someday he'll have to answer to God for it.

An unselfish person isn't out to make a haul. He's interested in caring about others. He'll probably end up in God's hall of fame instead of the hall of shame.

My prayer is that you stay focused on God and others and not on the things you want and ways to get what you want. The choice is yours. Which will it be, the hall of fame or the hall of shame?

Working It into the Week

Here are some verses you may want to have the kids look at during their personal devotions this week. Jot down the references on a separate sheet of paper for each of the kids.

Day 1: Luke 12:15-21

Day 2: Hebrews 12:1-3

Day 3: Matthew 19:21-22

Day 4: 1 Corinthians 10:24, 33

Day 5: Hebrews 13:5-6

Day 6: 1 Corinthians 13:4-5

Keeping Score

What's the Point?

In miniature golf the lowest score wins, so you could say that every stroke is a mark against you. We'll use this to point out that real love doesn't keep a list of wrongs.

Things You'll Need

- All you'll need is to find a nice miniature golf course nearby. This will be an easy one!

Here We Go

You can do this with just one child and yourself. It may be even more fun with three or four kids. Why not have your son or daughter invite some friends?

When you tell the kids you're taking them miniature golfing for devoes, I don't imagine you'll have many complaints, especially if you're going to a nice course.

Initially, you won't have to do anything for the devotions as far as the kids can see. Just play the game and keep score for each person like you normally would. At first, the kids may be trying to figure out exactly what devoes will be about, but after a bit they'll probably get wrapped up in the game.

While you're playing, observe how your kids react to each other's scores. Are they happy when a friend or sibling misses a shot and gets a higher score than they do? Also, try to take a mental note of how closely they watch each other's scores. Are they keeping track of each other's strokes and calling attention to someone if they don't think the person is counting his strokes accurately? "Hey, that wasn't a three! You took four strokes to get that one in!" You get the idea. This will give you some ammo to pull out later.

When the game is over, don't add up the final scores. Instead, find a good spot where you can sit down and talk about it as a family. You may want to hit a fast-food restaurant and get a snack. Once they're settled in with their snacks, you can start off by saying something like this:

Well, let's add up these scores and see who won.

You could let one of the kids do the adding. The others will probably be checking to be sure he's doing it right. As soon as the winner has been determined, say something like this:

You know, let me take another look at this. I'm thinking that maybe we were a little hard on (the name of the loser).

Now add the loser's score again, and do it out loud. This time throw out some of the big numbers. "It says that you got a six here, but that can't be right. Let's make it a three." Keep doing that until you get a negative reaction or some kind of protest from the others. As soon as you do, just move on with the devoes. You're doing fine.

Doing an accurate job of keeping score is pretty important in some cases, like in miniature golf. There are other times in life when keeping score is wrong. We tend to "keep score" on others, especially right here in our family. We always seem to know who did what wrong and how many times he did it, right?

Don't expect a "Gee, Mom or Dad, you're right." Not yet. You might get a smile out of them, or they may exchange knowing looks with each other. That's fine. Keep it rolling.

It's like we have this little mental list of the wrong things somebody else has done, and we use that list to our advantage whenever we need it. It goes something like this: I ask one of you to take out the garbage, and your first reaction may be to point out why someone else is more deserving of the job.

Here are some examples of this kind of score-keeping. You may want to tailor them to fit your family more closely.

- I ask you to do a chore and your response is: "Why are you asking me to do it? I already did some work for you, but (brother or sister's name) hasn't done a thing."

- Or maybe I have a talk with you about coming in late and I hear something like this: "(Brother or sister's name) was out late last night and you didn't say a word. Now I'm a little late and I'm in trouble. That's not fair!"

- Or maybe it's the phone. You're on the phone, I tell you I need it and after you hang up you complain about it: "Yesterday (brother or sister's name) was on the phone for an hour. Now today I'm on the phone for five minutes and I get yelled at."

- Or maybe it's something I hear going on between two of you:
  "You're always messing up my room."
  "You're always getting away with dodging the work."
  "You never let me work the TV remote."
  "You're always hogging the computer."

And the list could go on, right?

You can be sure they get the picture. Before they start trying to justify themselves, let's move on.

Did you know that this kind of stuff, this keeping score, is talked about in the Bible? It's called keeping a record of wrongs. It's a common thing, but it's deadly. It has no place in real love. Listen to how love is defined in First Corinthians 13:4-5:

> Love is patient, love is kind. It does not envy, it does not boast, it is not proud. It is not rude, it is not self-seeking, it is not easily angered, it keeps no record of wrongs.

Sooo, that means that if the Bible tells me I'm supposed to love others, but I keep a list of wrongs on them and keep pulling it out to my advantage, I'm not really loving the way I should. If I'm not loving the way God tells me to, then I'm sinning, right?

This was a mouthful. See if they got it.

Yeah, it all boils down to that. Someone can do something that I may feel is wrong, but if I keep a "list" on him instead of forgiving him, I'm in sin.

You know, this habit of keeping a record of wrongs gets more destructive the older you get. It can get really ugly in a marriage situation. It can turn a disagreement into a full-blown argument. It can build walls of resentment and hurt between people.

Jesus encountered the record-of-wrongs mentality all the time. The Pharisees kept a list of sorts on other people. They would criticize Jesus for associating with sinners. By their own lack of love, the Pharisees were being sinners themselves, even though they considered themselves to be pretty righteous guys.

Remember Mary and Martha? Jesus was visiting at their house. Mary was sitting at Jesus' feet while Martha was in the kitchen, fuming that her sister wasn't in there helping her. Martha pulled out the old record of wrongs and complained to Jesus. She expected Jesus to agree with her— after all, she was working so hard while Mary just sat around and visited! I imagine she was pretty surprised when Jesus pointed out that it was Martha's attitude that was the problem.

Does this make sense to you?

You can be almost certain they understand, regardless of any negative body language they may be giving you. This can be hard for them to hear, but it's something we are all guilty of, so it's definitely something they need to hear. Let's wrap it up quickly now.

Tie It Together

If God didn't really forgive us but kept a list of our "wrongs," then maybe we'd have an excuse for doing the same thing to others. But the fact is that when God forgives, He wipes the list clean. That's real love, and that's what He expects us to do for others.

I have to tell you, it works. I can tell you from personal experience that life is better when I'm not keeping the lists. Believe me. I still do it sometimes, because it's a natural tendency. But there is less stress and a lot fewer problems in my relationships with other people and in my life in general when I love the way God wants me to. That's what I want for you too. How can we all work on that?

We're trying to get them to think here. You've just been transparent with them and told them how you're working on not keeping score (and we all have to). Let's see if they really seem willing to give this a try too.

Watching the score in miniature golf is OK, but in real life, God wants us to quickly forgive each other when we get hurt or when someone wrongs us. He wants us to remember how much forgiveness He lavishes on us and then treat other people the same way. In other words, we need to tear up the score card.

Working It into the Week

Here are some references from the Bible that you may want to jot down on a separate piece of paper for each of the kids. You can give it to them after the devotions are done for use as a review during the week, or give it to them a week ahead of time as a prep for this family devotional.

Day 1: 1 Corinthians 13:4-5

Day 2: Psalm 103:8-14

Day 3: Luke 10:38-42

Day 4: Luke 7:36-50

Day 5: 1 Thessalonians 5:15

Day 6: Matthew 18:21-35

Shop 'til <u>They</u> Drop

What's the Point?

Putting the kids in a situation that will try their patience will give you a perfect opportunity to talk about being patient with others.

Things You'll Need

- All you'll need on this one is a little planning. The idea is to figure out an outing that the kids won't like and one that they will like. We're going to use shopping for this devotional as an outing the kids won't like, but we'll talk about some other alternatives in a minute. The idea is that you want the kids to come shopping with you and that, if there's enough time after you're done, you'll take them to a place they'd really like to go.

Sounds disastrous, doesn't it? That's the plan. The more bored they are with where you're shopping, the more impatient they'll become. That will lead us right into an aspect of love that we rarely work on: patience.

Alternate Ideas:

Don't be afraid to change the outing the kids won't like to suit your situation. If you're a mom, shopping may work great, especially if you have boys. If you have girls, shopping still works, but avoid any store or department that they might find interesting.

Here We Go

Start by getting the kids together and announcing your plans.

Hey, kids, later today we're going to have our family devotions, but before that there are some things I want to do. Then, if there's time, I'd like to take you to (tell them about the plans you have for them).

They should be excited about the activity or place you're going to take them. If they aren't, you'd better ask them what they'd rather do. Just switch gears and roll with it. If one kid likes your idea and another doesn't, you may have to incorporate more than one place to go so everyone is looking forward to it in some way.

Now, they may not have really heard the "catch," so you need to make sure it's clear.

Now, the thing is, I want to go to the store first, and if there is *time*, we'll go ahead and (go to the place they want to go, etc.).

If you hear some groans, that's really good. They're getting impatient already. Remember, it's very important that the kids go with you on the first part of the trip. This is a must. Explain that you'll go directly from the store to the place you're taking them, and besides, you really want to be with them.

Now, when you get to the store, take your time. Avoid a department the kids would have any interest in. If you're a mom, go look at the dresses. Stroll leisurely from rack to rack. Look at price tags. Try things on and look at the clothes on you as you slowly turn in front of the three-way mirror. You get the idea.

If you need to kill more time, check out the perfume or makeup counters. Don't feel like you need to buy a thing, and don't appear to be in any kind of hurry.

Now, hopefully the kids are getting noticeably impatient at this point. If they aren't, you have some unusual kids. They could probably teach the devoes on patience. Either way, you'll be able to illustrate patience when you wrap things up later.

The kids are probably watching the clock and realizing that you're cutting into their time. Whether or not you run out of time to do "their" activity is up to you. There is a fine line between impatience and exasperation. You don't want to cross the line and make them mad.

I'd say that when you've seen some obvious impatience displayed, you can pull the plug on your little charade and move on to doing the thing they're really looking forward to. If they showed even a little impatience earlier, you'll have all the material you'll need to talk about patience later.

After you've taken them to the place they were looking forward to going to, you'll need to wrap the devoes up for them. Say something like this:

OK, level with me on something. How did you feel when it took me so long to do my shopping?

I'm guessing they'll say they were anxious to get going to the part of the outing that they were looking forward to. They may not want to admit it just yet, but that's all right. (If your kids weren't impatient at all, you can still tie it in with a little positive reinforcement.) Let's move on with the devoes.

When you were looking forward to doing something you wanted to do, it was pretty hard to wait for me, wasn't it? After all, it was almost like I was cutting into your time, huh?

Hopefully you're getting some pretty open answers from them by now. You may even find out they were more impatient than you figured. That's often the case, which is why you want to make sure you don't drag the shopping part out too long.

Dads could choose to go to a hardware store, if you have girls. Instead of going shopping, you could just do some odd jobs or errands, but get the kids involved. Maybe you'll wash the car together and just when you finally dry it and the kids think you'll be ready to go to the activity they're excited about, tell them you think you'll wax the car too. It'll drive them nuts.

It will be easy to find something that will bore them. The harder and more important job is to find something they'll really want to do. It might be going to a sports store or an arcade for boys. Shopping at a department store may be just the ticket if you have girls, but you should obviously go to the department or store of their choice. Maybe the thing that will excite them is going out for ice cream or pizza or renting a movie. If they really like the idea, it shouldn't take them long to get impatient with whatever you choose to do first.

I can see how that situation tried your patience a little. That's exactly what I was hoping it would do, because I wanted to talk to you about being patient. Let me share some Bible verses with you:

> Be completely humble and gentle; be patient, bearing with one another in love. (Ephesians 4:2)

> And we urge you, brothers, warn those who are idle, encourage the timid, help the weak, be patient with everyone. (1 Thessalonians 5:14)

> Therefore, as God's chosen people, holy and dearly loved, clothe yourselves with compassion, kindness, humility, gentleness and patience. (Colossians 3:12)

Tie It Together

God is the perfect example of love, and a key element of love is patience. God is extremely patient, and He wants us to be patient too. Now, I'm sure all of you would agree that patience is important, right?

You're just tossing them a question to make sure that they're staying engaged in the devotional. Move on quickly.

Sure, patience is important. You all know that, yet in real life it gets really tough to put it into practice. Take today, for example. You were getting impatient with me, someone you love, because you wanted to do what you wanted to do more than you wanted to be patient with me—in truth, more than you wanted to love me at that time.

I know this sounds harsh, but it needs to be said. Say it nicely, of course. You don't have to sit there and accuse them. You simply want them to analyze it a little in a non-threatening way.

Hey, I'm not trying to say I'm perfect. I get impatient too, but that isn't the way God wants us to act. What do you think is at the very root of impatience?

You're fishing here, trying to make them think. Give them a moment, then move on.

I think impatience with others often boils down to pride. Think about it. If I'm impatient in traffic, if I want everyone to get out of my way so I can get to where I want to go, what does that really say about how I think of the people around me? It means that I'm considering my needs, my agenda, my schedule, to be more important than those of all the other people around me. In short, I'm acting as though I am more important than other people, and that is pride.

Just a little side note: If you're anything like most parents, you should be listening to this devotional too. We all have to work on our patience, don't you think? What's good for the kids is good for us too.

God demonstrates patience for us. He tells us in First Corinthians 13:4 that patience is a vital part of love. He definitely wants us to love others and to show part of that love by demonstrating patience. We all need to work on patience, don't you think?

A head nod is fine here. Move on.

What can we do to demonstrate patience with each other?

Let's see if you can get some input from them here. Pretty much any idea they give you will work. This is a good way of getting them to look for practical applications to biblical truths. And just wait—they might surprise you with some interesting insights into the subject. They most likely have the idea by now, so let's not try their patience any more today, eh? It's time to close.

Patience is something that we all need to work on. And, because patience isn't something that comes naturally to us, we need to ask for God's help on it. He has instructed us to love one another and one way we can demonstrate genuine love is by being patient with each other.

Working It into the Week

Here are some verses that deal with patience. Have your kids read them during the week. Just jot the references on a separate piece of paper for each of them. It would be good if you added these to your personal devotions this week too.

Day 1: 1 Timothy 1:15-17; 1 Thessalonians 5:14

Day 2: Ephesians 4:1-5

Day 3: James 5:10-11

Day 4: Galatians 5:22-23; Colossians 3:12-14

Day 5: Colossians 1:10-14

Day 6: Proverbs 14:29; 15:18; 16:32; 19:11

Kind Defined

What's the Point?

Doing something kind for others isn't very high on most kids' priority lists. We'd like to change that by giving them a chance to see how good it feels to do something kind for someone else.

Things You'll Need

- All you'll really need is to give this a little thought. Sound easy? Maybe.

Let me explain: In the devotional "Nip It in the Bud," found in this book on page 35, we addressed kindness from the aspect of treating people in a kind way instead of doing things that would hurt them. It was a reminder to be considerate of others. The point of the devotional, in short, was: Don't be mean.

In this devotional you'll be looking at kindness from a slightly different angle. Through this devotional, we want the kids to become proactive. We want them to look for opportunities to do something kind for others, ideally without the other person even being aware of it. This brings kindness to a higher level, and we want the kids to enjoy that experience.

Here We Go

There are a couple of ways to do this. You can do something kind for someone else together as a family, or you can have each family member come up with something kind to do on his own. If you do it as an entire family, just be sure you pick an act of kindness that everyone will enjoy.

I like the idea of encouraging each of the kids to think of an act of kindness on his own and then carry it out. A couple of kids may even want to buddy up together and work as a team. This would work especially well if you have children of varying ages. If they work as teams, the older children can help the younger ones.

We'll take the latter approach for this devotional. If you'd rather do something as an entire family, just modify the devoes to make it work.

When you're ready to talk to the kids, get them together and say something like this:

We've talked before about how we should be kind to others, whether or not we think they deserve it. But there's more to kindness than just biting your tongue when instead you'd like to bite someone's head off. We want to take kindness a step further and go out of our way to do something kind for someone.

Here's how we're going to do this: I'd like each of you to think of something kind you can do for a friend, a neighbor or someone in our family. You can do it entirely on your own, or you can buddy up with someone else in the family. Then, sometime this week I want you to follow through and do that kind thing for someone. If you want to do more than one thing, great. You must do at least one thing, though. Nobody gets off the hook on this one.

Next week we're going to get together and give each of you a chance to share what you did and how it made you feel, OK?

They may not be convinced that they even want to do this. Don't expect a lot of enthusiasm at this point. You may hear some excuses. They may think they're too busy, or they may feel that they have too much homework or that a job or sports will keep them from doing anything "extra," like being kind. That's OK. You have to be a rock on this. No exceptions. I mean, think about it: That's what happens to adults too, right? We often get too busy to do the little things that can really help and encourage others. So, let's make a point of doing our best to try to keep the kids from running into the same problem.

Now, let's brainstorm some things you may want to do for someone.

Get their input here. Have a pad of paper and start making a list to help them out. You should plan on doing something too, although some days your entire life is wrapped up in doing endless acts of kindness for the kids, right?

If the kids are bogging down when it comes to ideas, throw a couple out to get them thinking. You may want to make a list ahead of time. Here are a few we came up with:

- Wash the neighbor's car, mow his lawn, rake his leaves or shovel his drive, depending on the season.

- Bake cookies (with a little help from Mom) for someone.

- If you have an older neighbor, just stop by for a visit. Ask him to tell you some stories of when he first got married, or whatever you think he might enjoy telling you about. It would be a real act of kindness just to listen as he talks.

- How about making a phone call to someone you wouldn't normally call, or maybe writing a letter? Doing something

that would encourage that person would be a very kind thing.

- How about going to a friend's house and helping his or his parent with a project?

- You could help clean or dust for a neighbor.

- Help an elderly person go to the store.

- Babysit for a neighbor so he can go out.

- Help someone from school who struggles with his home-work.

Keep the list you made together handy so they can refer to it if they need to for ideas throughout the week.

When it comes to your act of kindness, break out of your routine a little. The things you normally do for your kids, while very kind, I'm sure, don't count.

Now, let's try to give the kids some inspiration before we end our little pow-wow today.

There is no finer example of being kind to other people in an active kind of way than the life of Jesus. He was kind to social outcasts, to the minorities, to the handicapped, to the people who were hurting and suffering. He was kind to the helpless and hopeless. He made life easier for a lot of people.

Jesus was always going out of His way to help others. The key is that it was an active kindness. He *did* something. In the ultimate act of kindness, He gave His life for those who didn't deserve it. He refused to get off the cross, although He could have.

Can you think of any other examples of Jesus being kind?

You may not get anything specific here, but as long as you can tell that they're thinking, it's OK.

Jesus could have pursued power and leadership among the people. Instead, the King of the Universe served people in kindness. Jesus is the definition of kindness. He is "kind" defined.

Let's follow Jesus' example and really work at being kind this week.

So far, so good. Now it's up to them. You may want to have them read the daily passages in the Bible that are listed in the Working It into the Week section as a way of getting themselves ready for performing their acts of kindness.

One more note on the act(s) of kindness you choose: Make sure you aren't forcing a sacrifice on the family without talking it over with them first. For example, if you chose to give a needy neighbor the money you were saving for a family vacation, your act of kindness really affects your family too.

As you go through the week, you may want to check to see how the kids are doing. It may be just the reminder they need. Don't go overboard on this to the point where you become an annoyance. We want them to experience the satisfaction of being kind. We don't want it to seem like an unwanted obligation.

Tie It Together

When the week is up, get the kids together and have them share about what they did. You can even share what you did. Be careful not to be critical of what they chose to do. Think of this as their first baby steps toward being more kind.

As each one shares, encourage them along. When they're done, you'll want to get their reactions to the whole thing. You might say something like this:

Now, tell me how performing this act of kindness made you feel? Were you glad you did it?

Hopefully you can get a little insight as to what is going on in their minds. You may need to ask more questions, such as: "How did the person react when you did the act of kindness for him?"

It sounds like doing these things for other people made you feel pretty good. But, remember, we don't do kind things for others just so that we feel good about ourselves. We do it because that's what Jesus did and we're to be like Him. We do it as an expression of love. We do it to be a good witness to what Jesus has done for us. The good feeling we get when we do something kind is just a bonus.

Active kindness doesn't always come naturally. It's a skill that we need to develop. God says that we're to love others. Love isn't simply a nice feeling we have inside for them. Love is action. Love demands that we do something. We need to ask God to open our eyes to the needs around us so that we can help in some way. Time invested in others like that is so much more satisfying than flopping on the couch and watching TV.

Here's a thought. Why not do it again? Have them do another act of kindness, something different from the first one, and share about it the next week. It would go a long way toward helping them adopt the proper mentality in their normal lives. If you like the idea, you might say something like this:

Doing kind things like this is important and will help you in years to come. Let's do this for one more week, OK? Do at least one more act of kindness for someone this week. Try to pick something different than you did the first week. We'll compare notes next week.

Encourage the kids along in this area. If you're proud of them, tell them. It may help prompt them to do more. Eventually we want them to know the satisfaction of being kind in an active way.

Working It into the Week

Here are some Scripture references that you may want to jot down on a separate piece of paper for each of the kids. Have them go over the verses during the week. The verses may prove to be inspiring as they think about doing something kind for someone this week.

Day 1: Mark 5:21-24; 6:56; John 4

Day 2: Mark 6:34-44; John 5:1-9

Day 3: 1 John 3:16-18

Day 4: Philippians 2:4-11; Hebrews 10:24

Day 5: John 13:34

Day 6: James 2:15-17

Riding on Rails

What's the Point?

We want to help illustrate what Jesus described as the two greatest commandments: loving God and loving your neighbor.

Things You'll Need

- This one's easy as far as prep time is concerned. You're going to take the family on a little train ride. I ended up taking a trip downtown into the city. You may want to check with the train line. Some have special "family" rates on weekends. It would also be nice to bring your camera and take a picture of the whole family on the train.

Here We Go

OK, make your plans for the train ride. You want to go someplace interesting for the kids. Downtown worked nicely for me. You might plan to hit a fun restaurant and maybe a museum, a big sporting goods store or something else that you think everyone will enjoy.

You may prep them in advance, telling them that you'll be riding the train for devoes this week. You may want to tell them to bring some money too, if you plan to hit a store they'd like.

When the day comes, take your train ride downtown and have a good time. I'd save your devoes talk for the ride home. If that doesn't work, tackle the lesson as soon as you get home.

You may want to start out with something like this:

You know, trains have been around for many generations. There have been a lot of changes to trains over the last hundred years, but one thing has pretty much stayed the same. Anybody think they know what I'm talking about?

Get some input from them. If they give you the answer you're fishing for, go ahead and move on. If not, help them out a little.

Well, it's not how the train is powered. That's seen some changes over the years. We don't see steam-engine trains anymore, right? I was thinking more along the lines of what the train runs on. The track, or rails.

Yeah, there have been plenty of changes to trains, but the track seems to have stayed pretty much the same. Trains still run on those two steel rails that lead all over the country.

So, how about a stupid question? What happens if the train slips off one of the rails?

This is an obvious question, but let them answer it anyway. If your kids are in their teens, you'll probably get a sarcastic answer. That'll work too. They're still going to get the point.

Right. If a train slips off even one of the rails, it's headed for disaster. Trains are designed to run on both rails, not one. Let me read a couple of Bible verses to you. This is how Jesus answered the man who asked him, "Teacher, which is the greatest commandment in the Law?" (Matthew 22:36).

> Jesus replied: "'Love the Lord your God with all your heart and with all your soul and with all your mind.' This is the first and greatest commandment. And the second is like it: 'Love your neighbor as yourself.' All the Law and the Prophets hang on these two commandments." (22:37-40)

Tie It Together

When Jesus was asked which of the commandments was the greatest, it was like asking Him to condense all of Scripture down to one fundamental principle. With all things considered, what did Jesus say were the most important things to do?

We just want to give them a chance to talk. They should come up with the answer easily enough. Now you want to flesh it out for them a little.

These two truths—loving God and loving your neighbor—are like the rails for a train. They're designed to be the track you travel on wherever you go. If you try to run on just one track, or only on the other, good luck. I can tell you that you won't get very far trying to run on just one rail. You need to love God, and you need to love people.

Some people think they'll do better without the guidance of either track. They are simply guided by doing whatever they want, without considering God or others. That formula won't work in the long run. Have you ever seen an "off-roading" train? Of course not. Trains aren't designed to run any place other than on the track. In the same way, God didn't design us to live just for ourselves. We're to love Him and love people.

Tell me what you think it means to love God with all your heart, soul and mind.

See what they say. Try to have them give you some examples. Loving God has a lot to do with willingly obeying Him too. Be sure that comes out, even if you have to bring it up. The fact is that if God tells us that there are some things He wants us to do that are very important to Him, how can we not obey Him if we truly love Him?

What about loving your neighbor? Give me some examples of how I can do that.

Now, if they ask, "Who is my neighbor?" take them right to Luke 10:29-37, the passage about the Good Samaritan, and show them that anyone in need is their neighbor. Hopefully they'll get some idea of how they should be treating others. This should affect how they treat kids at school, especially the ones who are not exactly the most popular kids in class.

You'll want them to know that loving "others" includes loving their siblings too. This may come as a shock to them. Let them know that loving others, like brothers or sisters, doesn't mean you love them only when they're being fair and reasonable to you. It means loving them all the time, whether you feel they deserve it or not.

Maybe you can share how you've been loving others lately. Explain to them how the principle of loving others affects your driving, for example. You know, how you always treat those tailgating "neighbors" with love. On second thought, maybe we ought to leave that one alone.

Loving God and loving others are like two rails or tracks that God designed us to run on. When we're riding squarely on those principles, there's almost no end to where we can go—just like a train.

We've had a good time riding the train today, but that wouldn't be the case if this train jumped the tracks. If a train derails, it will damage the train and potentially hurt every person riding in it.

If we derail, if we forget about loving God or our neighbors, we won't just be hurting ourselves. We'll be hurting all kinds of other people too. People who care for us. People who depend on us in some way.

Well, we've been laying it right on the line. You'll want to resist the tendency to get too preachy and just keep beating the same point over and over. They have a pretty good mental picture to hang on to. Any time you drive over some railroad tracks, the sound should serve as a reminder to them.

It's time to end this little devotional. You might ask them to give you a couple of ideas of ways they might try to love God more and show love to others more this week.

If you did take pictures during the day, get a copy made for each of them to use as a Bible bookmark or to put into a frame. It will serve as a little reminder of today's devoes.

Working It into the Week

Here are some Bible passages that will help reinforce this lesson. Jot the references down on a piece of paper for each of the kids and have them add it to their personal devotions this week.

Day 1: Mark 12:28-34

Day 2: 1 Corinthians 13:1-3

Day 3: 1 Corinthians 13:4-8

Day 4: Luke 10:29-37

Day 5: Matthew 7:12; Romans 13:8-10

Day 6: Galatians 5:13-15

Flying Under the Radar

What's the Point?

Pride is a terrible problem that has to do with "lifting oneself up." Pride gives you a big head, and in this devotional it will give you a wet one too.

Things You'll Need

- You can get by with a simple garden hose and one of those spray attachments for this devoes. You can substitute an arc sprinkler for the spray attachment if you'd rather. If you use the sprinkler, it needs to be adjustable so you can lock the water spray in one position instead of having it go back and forth. (Now, obviously, we don't want the children to freeze to death, so make sure that you do this devotional during warm weather.)

If you want to add a little extra atmosphere, go to your local library and pick up a CD or cassette tape of some steel-drum calypso music.

Here We Go

Get the hose set up with the spray attachment or the sprinkler. Test it out beforehand to make sure it works properly. Do you remember how the "limbo" game goes? You'll have the kids play a game of limbo today, but instead of going under a limbo pole, they'll have to duck under a stream of water.

Get the kids together and say something like this:

We're going to play a game of limbo today. Let's go outside and see just how low you can go.

Go outside and, if the kids aren't already familiar with the game, review how to play it. The object is to lean over backward to duck under the stream of water. When you're sure the kids understand how you're going to play, line them up and turn on the calypso music, if you have it. Start with the spray high, maybe head height, and let all the kids pass under it easily.

As they line up for another round, lower the hose just a little. As you repeat this procedure, the water stream will eventually get too low for someone. When they get a face full of water, they're eliminated from the game. In the end, the one who goes the lowest wins.

You may want to have a few towels ready for the wet heads. When the game is over, turn off the hose—or hang on to it if you want to stay dry! If you have teens around, they may try to turn this into a water fight. If it happens despite your best efforts, roll with it. You don't want to get impatient just before trying to convey some spiritual truths.

When the kids (and possibly you) have dried off, get them together and start off by saying something like this:

In life people generally think that the person who makes it to the "top" is the winner. In the game we played today, however, it was the person who managed to stay the *lowest* that came out ahead. When it comes to the area of pride, God's Word teaches that the person who raises his head in pride is the loser. Those who maintain a humble perspective are the ones who really get ahead in God's eyes.

Being humble is a rare thing. Pride is much more common, and it can be deadly. Listen to these verses that contrast pride and humility:

I know, there are a ton of verses here. I had a hard time cutting it down to this list. Read the whole list if you can, or pick the ones most appropriate for your kids.

Good and upright is the LORD;
    therefore he instructs sinners in his ways.
He guides the humble in what is right
    and teaches them his way. (Psalm 25:8-9)

When pride comes, then comes disgrace,
    but with humility comes wisdom.
                        (Proverbs 11:2)

The LORD detests all the proud of heart.
    Be sure of this: They will not go
        unpunished. (Proverbs 16:5)

Pride goes before destruction,
    a haughty spirit before a fall.
                      (Proverbs 16:18)

For whoever exalts himself will be humbled, and whoever humbles himself will be exalted. (Matthew 23:12)

Be completely humble and gentle; be patient, bearing with one another in love. (Ephesians 4:2)

Humble yourselves before the Lord, and he
will lift you up. (James 4:10)

Did one of these verses seem to stand out?

*We're looking for a little input here. If everyone is silent,
that's OK; just move on. You may get someone who mentions a
verse that really hit him, though. Listen to what he says. You may
be able to tie it in later. It's amazing how clear God's Word is
on the issue of the dangers of pride and the rewards of humility.
Hopefully, the kids are beginning to see that.*

If a fighter jet is flying in enemy territory, the
pilot will often fly extremely low to the ground to
avoid radar detection. His very life may depend
on his ability to fly under the radar.

The same thing happens with us. When we
start lifting our heads in pride, we're flying in
enemy territory. The enemy is the devil, and pride
has long been one of his trademarks. Just like a
pilot being in real danger when he is detected by
enemy radar, pride puts us in harm's way.

In the verses we read, pride was associated
with words like *destruction*, *punishment* and *disgrace*. Not very good things, huh?

*See what they say. Of course they agree, even if they don't
express it. Keep going.*

Tie It Together

The attitude of pride has to do with me feeling
like I'm more important than others. It's a lifting
up of myself. It brings attention to me. It is the
idea that what *I* want to do is the most important thing, that what *I* think is all that counts
and that what really matters is how *I* feel. It's
that "how dare somebody treat me that way?"

attitude that we've discussed in other devotionals. It's "me first" all the way.

An attitude of humility, however, is just the opposite. A humble person puts others' needs and wants ahead of his own. He cares about how others feel. Humility keeps life in perspective. It isn't an inferiority thing at all. A humble person realizes that God made him, loves him and wants him to love others. A humble person understands that there is no legitimate basis for pride. God made us, gave us life and gave us abilities and opportunities. If I'm going to be proud, I should be proud of God, not myself.

What are some things people tend to be proud of?

Let's see what they say here. Things like "looks," "body," "abilities," "talents," "things" and "intelligence" can make the list, to name a few. After they've given some input, let's wrap it up for them. We've been circling the field; now it's time to put the landing gear down.

Most of the good things people take pride in would have been impossible without God. He gives us our looks, our bodies, our brains. He gives us life and health to develop talents and abilities, to get jobs and to be able to afford things.

Pride is really kind of foolish, when you think about it. And worse than that, it's dangerous. When we let pride into our hearts, we're playing in the devil's playground. God is obligated to hold back His blessings from the proud and even punish them if He so decides. Does that make sense?

Give them a moment to process what you just said. If they give you some input, great. Otherwise, move on.

Being humble is having a servant attitude. It rejects the attitude of "the world revolves around me." A humble person doesn't seek to lift himself up. He flies "under the radar." He's not out to get noticed or to get a lot of attention. He's not eager to claim all the credit. He tends to give credit where credit is due. The credit for things should go to God, don't you think?

If they answer, great. If not, you can be sure they're thinking. Your wheels are down; it's time to land this thing.

We all wrestle with pride. I do, and every person I know does. I can be humble one moment, then filled with pride the next. It's a battle. It's something we have to pay attention to and work on. God resists the proud, but gives grace to the humble. God rewards us when we do it right. Let's work at staying humble and try to "fly under the radar," OK?

Working It into the Week

Here are some verses that warn against pride and encourage us to have humble attitudes. Jot down the references on a separate piece of paper for each of the kids and have them add it to their personal devotions this week. This is great stuff!

Day 1: Psalm 18:27; 25:9; James 4:10

Day 2: Proverbs 11:2; 13:10; 16:5, 18

Day 3: Proverbs 18:12; 29:23; Titus 3:1-2

Day 4: Isaiah 66:2; Matthew 11:28-30

Day 5: Matthew 23:12; Ephesians 4:2

Day 6: Matthew 18:1-4; Philippians 2:3; Colossians 3:12; 1 Peter 5:5-6

Nothing but the Truth

What's the Point?

Our culture is trying to shed the idea that there is absolute truth. We'll use a watermelon and gravity to remind the kids that there are absolutes.

Things You'll Need

- Pick up a nice big watermelon. I wouldn't settle for one of those half ones. If watermelons are out of season and you really want to do this devotional now, you can substitute the watermelon with tomatoes or anything else that will burst when you drop it from the second story of a building.

- Now, if you want to get a little more participation from the kids, pick up a dozen eggs too.

- You need to find a place you can drop the watermelon and the eggs from. The higher the better. A bridge crossing the highway is strictly taboo. If you have a two-story house or know someone who does, dropping from a second story window may be perfect if there is a hard surface below.

Here We Go

Some people say there is no such thing as absolute truth. They say that something might be true for you, and something totally different might be true for someone else.

In some cases, they're right. My favorite dinner may be spaghetti, but it isn't everybody's favorite dinner. The truth about favorite dinners is that it's different for everybody.

Many people want to take this "truth is different for everybody" philosophy to the extreme. They go way beyond "opinion" issues like favorite foods. They want to discard "absolute truth" altogether. Why do you think that is so important to some people?

Let's see what they say here. I wouldn't expect them to get it just yet, but they may come close.

I would guess that it's a pretty selfish motive. If there is no absolute truth, people can pretty much do what they want without feeling guilty about it. If there is no absolute truth, then there really isn't any right or wrong either.

That means that the Bible is just a nice book, but that you're under no real obligation to believe or obey what it says. Does that make sense?

You want to make sure they're tracking with you here. If not, try to rephrase it so they get it before you move on.

Some people have gotten to the point where they refuse to believe that there are any absolutes at all. The truth is, there are plenty of absolutes, and we're going to look at one right now.

Grab the watermelon and eggs and head to that second-story window.

The law of gravity: There's an absolute for you. If I hold this watermelon out of the window and let go, it will surely go down. Does anybody disagree with me?

OK, if you have teenagers, they may disagree, even with the law of gravity. They probably want to make sure you'll really drop the watermelon. Now, if the kids can handle it safely, you may want to let one of them do the dropping. I know, I know. You were looking forward to making the drop, right? Well, hey, the kids will get more out of it if you let them do it. The others may want to go outside and watch, but preferably not directly below the window.

Set it up however you want. You may even stand outside and take a picture. It will be a great reminder about this lesson. After the watermelon crashes to the ground, pull out the eggs. Everybody should get a couple of turns this time—even you. When you've dropped all the ammo, get the kids together and move right to the application. Save the cleanup for later.

Gravity. It's an absolute truth, and I don't think anybody will argue with you on that. That alone destroys the theory that there is no absolute truth. More important than gravity is the God who created it. Listen to some of these verses:

> Jesus answered, "I am the way and the truth and the life. No one comes to the Father except through me." (John 14:6)

> "If you hold to my teaching, you are really my disciples. Then you will know the truth, and the truth will set you free." (John 8:31-32)

> For the time will come when men will not put up with sound doctrine. Instead, to suit their own desires, they will gather around them a great number of teachers to say what their itching ears want to hear. They will

turn their ears away from the truth and turn aside to myths. But you, keep your head in all situations, endure hardship, do the work of an evangelist. (2 Timothy 4:3-5)

Tie It Together

There *is* absolute truth. The people of this world don't want to believe that. They want to make you believe that there is no truth that is true for everybody. They want to be able to do whatever they feel like doing without thinking God will judge them for it. Well, they can believe whatever they want, but that belief alone doesn't make what they believe true.

Some people don't want to admit that the Bible is absolute truth. If you try to tell them that it is absolute truth, they will argue with you or tune you out. It's like they jam their fingers in their ears. They don't want to hear the truth. If there truly is sin and only one way to heaven, and if God will judge all their thoughts and actions someday, well, that would mean they would have to change. They don't want to do that. They'd rather believe in the "there is no absolute truth" philosophy.

The sad thing is that by rejecting the truth of the Bible, they miss out on so much. They don't have the comfort of knowing that God loves them, that He offers complete forgiveness, that He wants to adopt them as His children and heirs and that He promises to never leave or forsake His own.

Where do you think this whole "there is no absolute truth" idea came from?

You've been doing all the talking here, so you should wrap it up quickly. They'll probably guess that the theory was born in hell. If they see that, great. If not, point it out to them.

Yeah, I would guess that the devil started that whole line of thinking. The tragedy is that a lot of people are buying it. But we want you to know the truth. Just like the law of gravity, absolute truths really do exist. The Bible is at the top of the list. Be careful that nobody steals the truth of that statement from you, OK?

One last thought: You may have friends who have bought into the devil's lie. Pray for them. Share your faith with them. Listen to this verse:

> My brothers, if one of you should wander
> from the truth and someone should bring
> him back, remember this: Whoever turns a
> sinner from the error of his way will save
> him from death and cover over a multitude
> of sins. (James 5:19-20)

Genuine love tells the truth. God loves us so much that He gave His son for us. He also gave us the Bible to show us the true way to heaven and happiness.

It's time to end it. They've gotten the basic message, you can be sure of that.

Working It into the Week

You may want to take the verses below, jot them on separate pieces of paper for each of the kids and have them add them to their personal devotional times this week.

Day 1: Psalm 31:1-5; John 14:6

Day 2: Matthew 22:15-16; 25:31-46

Day 3: John 1:14, 17; 6:46-51

Day 4: John 8:31-32, 42-47; 2 Timothy 4:3-5

Day 5: John 8:51; 18:37; Acts 20:30-31; Romans 1:18-25

Day 6: Psalm 25:4-5; 86:11; 119:30-33; Ephesians 6:13-14; 1 Timothy 2:1-6; 2 Timothy 2:15

When the Going Gets Tough . . .

What's the Point?

Just as athletic ability doesn't come without discipline, practice and a lot of hard work, genuine love can't reach its intended potential without a similar type of perseverance.

Things You'll Need

- All you'll need to do is to decide on a sporting event to attend. Any sport will do. Basketball, volleyball, football, soccer, track or golf, to name a few. Pick a sporting event that your kids would be interested in. That's important. It may be badminton or bowling, wrestling or skateboarding—it doesn't matter what the sport is as long as the kids will enjoy watching it. If you have girls that are into figure skating, take them to a figure skating competition.

You don't have to spend a lot of money on the sporting event. Local park district leagues or high school teams would work fine. If you want to go to a pro game, that's great too.

Now, if sports of any kind are simply not where your kids are at, you can easily work out an alternative activity. The question is, what are they into? If they're into cooking, try getting a tour of a restaurant's kitchen somewhere. If they're into some kind of career field, try to arrange for an interview and a tour. If they're really

Here We Go

If you've picked a sporting event your kids will really enjoy, they ought to be pretty excited when you announce your plans. Go to the event and enjoy. You don't have to worry about teaching them a thing during the game.

When the event is over, the kids may be wondering how it will tie in to family devoes, but they won't be complaining on the way home. Once you get home, you can start off the devotional with something like this:

We saw some pretty talented players today. How many years do you suppose some of them have trained to compete as well as they did?

You'll have to tailor the questions to the event you attended. Answers will vary depending on whether the event you saw was at the amateur or pro level, but the kids will still probably say the training took years. Good, you're on your way.

Years of training. Tell me what you think would have been involved in their training.

You can answer the question, but it's better to have them do the thinking—it keeps their minds in gear. Now repeat what they tell you and add some of your own thoughts if you'd like.

They would need weight training to build their strength and hours and hours of practice to develop their skills. They'd need good coaching too.

Do you think they ever had setbacks during all that training?

It's almost a ridiculous question, but ask it anyway. Sometimes when kids see a talented athlete, they forget how much effort the individual had to put in to become that good at the game.

Sure, there are always setbacks. Injuries, failures, disappointments and mistakes are always a part of developing a skill like that. Do you think there were times when some of the players we saw today might have thought about quitting?

We want them to think this one through too. They may not have considered it before, but almost every accomplished athlete has thought about quitting at some point or another.

I'm sure every athlete has been tempted to give up or quit at some point. That's a very natural reaction, especially when they're tired or discouraged. The fact that we saw them on the field today is evidence that they've shown some real determination to keep going. Call it whatever you like—endurance, commitment, discipline or perseverance—without it you can't make it in athletics or any other area of interest. Would you agree with that?

We just want them to digest that point. It's the old "no pain, no gain" principle. If you just get a nod of the head, fine. Move on.

It's no different in the Christian life. God loves us in a committed, enduring way. He expects our love for Him and our love for others to have a growing element of perseverance to it. Love without a strong commitment is weak and flabby. It's like Jell-O. God wants our love to be strong, to endure like granite.

I love the story in First Samuel 30 about David and his men. They were returning home after a long three-day march only to find that their town had been raided and burned by an enemy. The men's wives and children had been taken captive and were nowhere in sight.

David and his men were discouraged and wept until they didn't have the strength to cry

into music, take them to see a band or orchestra. You get the idea. It doesn't have to be athletics.

anymore. The men who had made David their leader held him responsible and were ready to kill him. It would have been a tragic end to the story of David. But the story goes on to say that David found strength in the Lord his God.

He rallied the men to pursue the raiders who now had a huge head start on them. The men were so exhausted that 200 of them were left behind at one point when they didn't have the strength to cross a ravine.

David and his 400 remaining men caught up to the raiding Amalekites and found them celebrating their victory. David and his men attacked them as the sun was going down. The battle raged on all night and the next day. By that evening they had totally defeated the enemy raiding party and had rescued their wives and children. Not one wife or child had been lost. It's a fantastic story of perseverance. It's a story that demonstrates how real love must keep going and never quit.

Tie It Together

There's an old saying, "When the going gets tough, the tough get going." The truth is, when the going gets tough, most people head for the door. Problems, discouragement and tough times can often drive people to quit.

As Christians, we have been commanded to love God and to love others. That love is described in First Corinthians 13. The description ends with these words: "It always protects, always trusts, always hopes, always perseveres. Love never fails" (13:7-8).

You may have a personal story that you can inject here of a time you really "hung in there" and you're glad you did. You could also share a story of a time when you quit and how you're sorry that you did. This is powerful stuff. The kids need to hear about it.

We can keep going on this topic for a long time. There are so many biblical examples, good and bad, but you'll have to resist the urge to talk too much. It's better to end with the kids wanting more than the other way around. After devoes are officially over, if the kids want to discuss other personal examples of people they know, great.

I got some good advice once. The person told me that it isn't always the most talented people who make it to the top, but rather it's the persistent ones—the ones who keep going. I've found that to be true.

It's certainly true in the Christian life, particularly in the area of love. We have to love God through the hurts and disappointments and setbacks of life. We have to love others even when we don't feel that they treat us right. This is essential in relationships. I can't stress it enough.

Did you ever notice that they don't make tombstones out of cardboard? They make them out of granite. Freezing cold, scorching heat, wind, rain and storms come and go, and still the granite stands. We don't want to be weak, "cardboard Christians" when it comes to loving God and loving others. We want to be like granite. We want to hang in there, to endure. Just as in sports, perseverance in the Christian life is essential. There will be failures, disappointments and hardships. But we need to be strong and remember it will all be worth it if we keep going.

God has designed a race for each of us to run as Christians. Our goal is to become more like Jesus. We want to love God and others with a never-gonna-quit kind of love. God doesn't want you to be a spectator. He wants you to get in the race.

I think they have it. Go ahead and wrap things up.

Working It into the Week

Encourage them to add these verses to their daily personal devotional times:

Day 1: 1 Samuel 30

Day 2: 1 Corinthians 13:7-8

Day 3: Romans 5:1-5

Day 4: James 1:2-4

Day 5: 2 Peter 1:5-9

Day 6: Matthew 7:24-27; Hebrews 12:1-3

Protector or Defector

What's the Point?

We'll use a dozen eggs to illustrate to the kids the dangers of bailing out on one of the frequently forgotten duties of love: protecting those we love.

Things You'll Need

- You'll be going to the grocery store with the kids for this one. All you'll really need is two cartons of eggs. Now, don't get nervous; this isn't going to be very messy. Each carton should contain one dozen large grade-A eggs. (More about that in just a bit.)

- You'll also need to plan a meal that will use a good number of eggs. It could be scrambled eggs, an omelette or french toast. Be sure you have all the ingredients you'll need for the meal you choose.

Here We Go

You'll want to time this so you can go to the store and get the eggs and still have enough time to make the meal when you get back.

Get the kids together for devoes and announce that you're all going to the grocery store for the first part of family devoes. You might want to bring enough extra money to let each of them pick up a bottle of soda or juice to drink during devoes.

Once you're in the store, go right to the cooler where they have the eggs. You might have one of the kids help you pick a couple of cartons. Be sure they open the cartons to briefly check that none of the eggs are cracked or broken.

Now that you have the eggs, you're ready to head to the checkout line. The kids are probably wondering what you're planning to do with all those eggs. Don't tell them if they ask. Let them wonder.

If you do let the kids get some kind of treat or drink for themselves, don't let them eat or drink it until you start your devoes at home.

In the checkout line, be sure you get a separate plastic bag for each of the two cartons of eggs. If you pick up any other grocery items in the store, don't put them in the bags with the eggs.

When you get to the car, put one of the bags of eggs down on the ground and take the carton out. You might say something like this:

We aren't going to use the carton for this dozen eggs; we'll just carry them in the bag. One of you hold open the bag for me, will you?

When one of the kids opens the bag, you'll want to open the egg carton and dump the eggs in. You want some eggs to crack and break when you do this, so don't be too careful. You'll have to fight your instincts on this one. It will be interesting to see the kids' reactions.

Pack the eggs and the kids into the car and head home. You'll have to watch how you put the bag of unprotected eggs in the car. You don't need them oozing onto the seat or carpet.

Plan to get right into the devotional when you get home. Gather the kids around the table and let them open their juice or soda. Don't worry about them spoiling their dinner. Sometimes kids listen better when they have something to snack on or drink while you talk.

Put the carton of eggs on the table and open it up. Ask one of the kids to inspect the eggs for cracks or breaks just like they did at the grocery store. All of the eggs should still be intact.

Next, it's time for the unprotected eggs. Put a big bowl on the table and pour the eggs in it. Hopefully, some of the eggs are broken and the yokes are dripping from the bag.

OK, so we've had a little damage to this dozen. Can you tell me how many eggs are broken or damaged?

Let the kids try to get a quick count. All you're doing here is emphasizing the fact that unprotected eggs are going to get damaged.

Who can tell me what the purpose of the carton was?

The answer is pretty obvious, but sometimes kids will look at it as a trick question. If they start reaching for some answer other than the obvious, rephrase the question. You could say, "What did the carton do for this dozen eggs?" and point at the unbroken dozen. They should come up with something remotely like "protect the eggs." That's what you're looking for, so keep going.

Right, the egg carton is designed to protect the eggs. These eggs probably traveled hundreds of miles by truck before they got to the grocery store, and this little carton kept them safe and protected. When we took the carton away and traveled just a few miles to get these home, some of the eggs got broken.

What are these broken eggs good for now? I'd probably toss them out before I'd try to pick all the bits of broken shells out of here. Without the basic protection the eggs were designed to get from a simple carton, I lose a lot of the eggs.

This reminds me a lot of life. Did you know that God gave us some basic "egg carton" responsibilities? First Corinthians 13 tells us that we're to protect those we love. How do we do that?

Here's where it gets tricky. It can be tough to get their input at this point. They may be quiet at first, but that's OK. Give them a moment to process the question. If you still don't get a response, rephrase the question or "prime the pump" with an example.

Does protecting someone I love mean that I "cover" for him when he is involved in something wrong?

Well, that question may open a can of worms, but it may also help get a discussion going.

"Covering" for someone may be the opposite of protecting someone. It may keep him from facing the consequences of his choices and may allow him to go deeper into sin.

Protecting someone you love is like being a conscience for that person. You want to help encourage him to stay on the right path for his own protection and well-being. If I truly love someone, I have to be willing to stand up to him to keep him from going in directions God would not want him to go.

Maybe someone I love is hanging around the wrong kids and some of their bad influence is wearing off on him. I need to protect the one I'm supposed to love by saying something to him, don't I? First Corinthians 15:33 tells us that "bad company corrupts good character." Do I want someone I'm supposed to love to get corrupted without me trying to protect him?

I don't know if they'll respond verbally, but their minds will definitely be working.

What about a friend or brother or sister who is watching movies or listening to music that isn't good for him? God says love obligates you to protect him. How would you do it?

We're trying to get them to understand that they can't be spectators when it comes to protecting others. They have to get involved. Any attempt is better than no attempt at all.

How else do we need to protect others?

Their wheels are turning now. See what they say. Take whatever they give you and build on it.

Protecting those we love has to do with keeping them from doing things that will harm them, whether it's their choices, attitudes or whatever. It also has to do with protecting them from harm from others. What do I mean by that?

Wait for some responses and then run with them. Add to it as you see the need.

When others say things that hurt someone you love, you can balance it out by encouraging that person and building him up. Give me an example of how you might do that.

I'd expect they may struggle a little with an answer here. Help them along.

When you see that someone you love is hurting, treat him how you would like to be treated if a similar thing happened to you. You might be able to see the situation a little clearer and be able to help him grasp the big picture. Also, never underestimate the power of Scripture. Sometimes just jotting down a verse or two for someone can help him keep his perspective, and it protects him in a very real sense.

Sometimes, the people we love need protection from us. Sometimes we're the ones who hurt them; we're the ones who tear them down when we should be building them up. We're dumping extra baggage on them when we should be helping them shoulder the load. Does that make sense to you?

Well, you may not have the kids straining to give input on how they might harm someone they love, but I'm sure the Lord may be convicting them at this moment. The truth is that we do it ourselves sometimes too, don't we?

Tie It Together

When it comes to people in our own family, sometimes the person we're supposed to protect is really acting like a jerk. It's hard to concern ourselves with protecting him when he's like that.

We need to remember that God wants us to be "bodyguards" to those we should love, even when they don't seem to deserve it. God isn't finished with any of us yet. He wants to make each of us into a masterpiece. Sometimes we have to look beyond what a person is like at this moment and try to look at him from God's perspective.

Jesus makes this concept very clear in Matthew 5:43-48. He tells us that we're supposed to love our enemies no matter what. So, if I'm only loving those who treat me great, what's the big deal with that? Anybody can do that. As Christians, we're to love others even when they don't "deserve" it.

There's a great story in First Samuel 25 about a women named Abigail. Unfortunately, Abigail was married to a real jerk named Nabal. Nabal was greedy and arrogant. He refused to give food to David and his men after they had protected Nabal's herds. David got so mad that he took 400 men with him for the purpose of attacking and killing Nabal and his servants. But Abigail heard what happened and quickly arranged for a huge amount of food to go to David and his men. She protected Nabal, even though he clearly didn't deserve it.

Next, Abigail met David and his men on the way. She offered them the food and asked that they spare her husband. She begged David not to take things into his own hands, but to leave them in the Lord's. She did not want him to look back on this day with regret and guilt. At this point, David was like an enemy to her, yet she was trying to protect him. David listened and realized that what she said was true. Abigail helped protect him from terrible sin and regret.

God rewarded Abigail in an unusual way for trying to protect others.

I bought eggs to make (tell them the meal you have planned for them). The eggs in this bowl won't make much of a contribution to that meal.

They weren't protected, and so they can't provide as much for others to enjoy as the eggs that were protected in the carton.

You need to remember that idea as you live here in this family and as you have families of your own someday. If you tear each other down, if you fail to protect each other, everybody loses something. But when you protect each other, there will be benefits to you and the one you try to protect.

Let's be bodyguards for each other. We need to realize that, like an egg, we're all pretty easily damaged.

God says it's our responsibility to protect those we love. If we try to dodge this duty, we become "defectors" of sorts to one of the real duties of love. Let's ask God to help us be protectors, not defectors, OK?

We went a little long here. Streamline it if you can. Believe me, they understand the concept. Putting it into practice is the hard part. Ask God how you can demonstrate this aspect of love throughout the week.

Now, it's time to get that meal cookin'. Hey, it's one more example of how good things come out of a little protection.

Working It into the Week

Here are some references you may want to jot down on a separate piece of paper for each of the kids. Have them add it to their personal devotions as a reminder about our duty to protect each other.

The verses for the kids' personal devotions start with the story about Abigail and David. This is a great example of how love can protect. Then we move on to the fact that God protects those He loves. The kids will read Jesus' prayer for the protection of those He loves. We review First Corinthians 13 to show that real love protects others, and then we have a number of verses reminding us to love others.

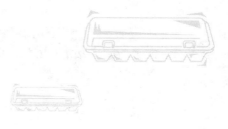

Day 1: 1 Samuel 25

Day 2: Psalm 32:7; 37:28; 41:1-2; 91:14

Day 3: John 17:11-15

Day 4: 1 Corinthians 13:4-7; 1 Thessalonians 4:9-10

Day 5: 1 Peter 3:8-12; 4:8

Day 6: John 15:12-13; Romans 12:9-10; Ephesians 5:1-2; 1 John 3:16; 4:19-20

Other Books
by Tim Shoemaker

Tried and True Job

Wearing the Mask

Smashed Tomatoes, Bottle Rockets
. . . and Other Outdoor Devotionals You Can Do With Your Kids

Mashed Potatoes, Paint Balls
. . . and Other Indoor/Outdoor Devotionals You Can Do With Your Kids

Reboot Your Brain